I0815840

THE COMMON SENSE COWBOY'S GUIDE TO LIFE

THE COMMON SENSE COWBOY'S GUIDE TO LIFE

STORIES FROM THE OLD GUY AT THE END OF THE BAR

PATRICK DORINSON

WITH MATHEW KLICKSTEIN

Humanix Books

www.humanixbooks.com

Humanix Books

The Common Sense Cowboy's Guide to Life

Humanix Books, P.O. Box 20989, West Palm Beach, FL 33416, USA
www.humanixbooks.com | info@humanixbooks.com

Cover and Interior Author Photo: Aaron Phelps, Mile 21 Photography

Interior Art:

Bourbon Glass: iStock/Azure-Dragon

Good Guys Wear White Hats by John Falter: Alamy/Retro AdArchives

Cowboy Hat Icon: iStock/Mary Desy

Cover and Interior Design: Ben Davis

ISBN: 978-1-63006-335-1 (Hardcover)
ISBN: 978-1-63006-336-8 (E-book)

Printed in the United States of America
10 9 8 7 6 5 4 3 2 1

This book is lovingly dedicated to the two most important people in my life, my mother and father.

To my mother, who bore me, nurtured me, taught me, encouraged me, scolded me when I needed it, and through the stories of her childhood on her sister's ranch, set my feet on the path that has led me to the cowboy way.

To my father, whose wise counsel throughout my life, patience with my shortcomings, valiant attempts to teach me math, and unfailing optimism showed me how to live a life with purpose.

But most of all, for the love they gave me, which has sustained me all these years.

I wish they were here to read this book because without them I never would have been able to write it.

Every day in the saddle's a good day.

CONTENTS

FOREWORD

The book of Ecclesiastes said, "There is nothing new under the sun." That may have been true at the time the Bible was written but certainly not true today. With the expansion of knowledge have come the expansion of problems but also the expansion of solutions. The expansion of conflicts but also the expansion of peace. The expansion of ignorance but also the expansion of intelligence.

And with all this also comes the expansion of advice—often bad but sometimes good. Religious advice is good. Gang advice is bad. Parental advice is good.

Advice from someone like Benjamin Franklin has proven to be good down through the ages. Advice from someone like Aaron Burr is not to be followed, as it has proven to be the wrong way to go.

Some books give good advice, some bad. This book, *The Common Sense Cowboy's Guide to Life*, gives good advice—something you might want to read, absorb, and put into practice.

We all encounter rough seas on the ocean of life. That is inevitable. It's not just that stormy seas come, it's how we handle them as we attempt to sail into the quiet and peaceful harbors we all desire.

As the authors of The Federalist Papers—Hamilton, Madison, and Jay—said, being a good president is all about character. And that is good for all of us. It comes down to character. Knowing when to say "Yes" and "No" and knowing the right way to do things and the wrong way to do things.

I hope that, in reading the book before you, you may acquire a few more strategies for how to avoid the bad things, do the good things, and, hopefully, have a few laughs along the way.

Craig Shirley

THE SECRET TO A LONG LIFE
IS GETTING UP EVERY DAY WITH A PURPOSE.
YOUNG OR OLD, WORKING OR RETIRED,
EVERYONE NEEDS A PURPOSE, SO FIND YOURS.

JOHN FALTER

Little boy, born in the city
His heroes were always John and Roy
He'd watch them every Saturday
At the afternoon matinee
All he wants is just to be a cowboy
Born too late, born in the city
In his dreams, he still rides with John and Roy
Toy gun and holster on his hips
Ridin' horses made of sticks
All he wants is just to be a cowboy
In his dreams, all he needs is a good horse beneath him
And in his dreams, all he needs is the open range to keep him
And in his dreams, he's ridin' fences
A young man workin' in the city
His heroes were always John and Roy
In a 10-story high rise, in polished shoes and neckties
All he wants is just to be a cowboy
In his dreams, all he needs is a good horse beneath him
And in his dreams, all he needs is the open range to keep him
And in his dreams, he's ridin' fences
One day, they found a note on his desk that read:
"I gotta clear m'head
I gotta go where I can breathe the air
You'll find me there"
Now he's gone
All he owns is his hat, chaps and lasso
And he smiles
As he ties his bedroll upon the saddle
And he dreams of a peaceful sleep
And he prays his soul to keep
On ridin' fences

—"Riding Fences," The Travelling Mabels

INTRODUCTION

WHEN YOU'RE RUNNING OUT OF SUNSETS, DON'T WASTE THE SUNRISES YOU HAVE LEFT.

A man isn't born a cowboy. He becomes one.

Well . . . *I* wasn't born a cowboy.

In fact, I wasn't born on a ranch or in the cowboy country of the great American West.

I was born in suburban California.

But if the "cowboy way" can be transmitted through DNA, I *do* come by it honestly.

My mother spent a good part of her childhood at her older sister Kate's Parkview Ranch near Rand, Colorado. Kate, together with her husband, Bryant, raised cattle and some sheep.

They all lived in a log house.

She learned how to ride from a full-blooded Cheyenne Indian.

She learned how to work cows and took care of the bummer lambs who had been abandoned by their mamas.

She had a big ol' dappled gray horse named Skeezix.

And during the summer, she would pack supplies up to the sheep camp by herself.

Mom was small in stature, but the cowboys liked her "spunk," and they taught her all they knew.

Towards the end of her life, I would visit her, and we would sit and engage in some small talk. It was difficult, as her memory was fading.

But whenever I mentioned the ranch, horses and cowboys, her steel gray eyes would light up and she would vividly tell me in rich detail the stories she had filled my head with since I was a small boy.

When she died, a large piece of me died, as well.

During that tough time, I was in a career rut and unhappy. I asked myself: *What would SHE want me to do with my life?*

Then I remembered what she had told me she had done when her dad died, and she had been all by herself—an eighteen-year-old country girl working as a domestic in someone else's home.

She said she had looked into the mirror in her small room and told herself, "Well, Jeanne, *it's up to you now*."

If I wanted to change the path of my life, it was up to *me* now.

A man can master many things in life, but it takes a long time to know who you really are inside.

Some folks never find out. *I* was *determined* to find out.

I didn't know it at the time, but I needed to "cowboy up."

If you do an Internet search on the term "cowboy up," you'll find many different definitions, most of them written by people who probably have no idea what the phrase actually means.

Real cowboys and cowgirls know *exactly* what it means (and when to use it). And sometimes it's not spoken. It can be a piercing look, a knowing nod, or a tip of the hat.

Most of the cowboys I know are folks of few words; although, when they *do* talk, you better listen carefully, because they probably won't chew their words twice.

"Cowboy up" can't be taught . . . you must learn it.

To cowboy up means you're facing not just your fears, but also *anything* that's in front of you, any time you're met with a challenge. You're going to face many challenges in your life from the moment you struggle to take that first breath until you give up the struggle for life and breathe your last. But you gotta *face* them by yourself. It's on you.

Anything in life where you either mentally or physically learn to do something new will be a challenge.

So, what are you gonna do? Are you gonna *avoid* that challenge? Are you gonna figure a way out of it? Or are you gonna say to yourself, "I gotta cowboy up, I gotta look this right in the eye, and I gotta solve it.

It helps to have someone who knows what "cowboy up" means and can "learn" you.

I found that person in Idaho.

Trudy Peterson is a born and bred cowgirl, and when we met, she immediately reminded me of my mother, and I knew in an instant that we were meant to meet.

She has become a dear friend, and on more than one occasion she has "learned" me to cowboy up while at the same time teaching me the "cowboy way."

Like the time when she was showing me how to better work with my horse Beamer. She would tell me about the connection between horse and rider and how it was key so that he and I could work together better.

When I got it right, and Beamer perfectly, or damn-near perfectly, executed the maneuver, I was asking him to do, she would ask, "Do you feel that?" At first, I didn't know what she meant. I didn't know what I was supposed to feel.

Then it made sense. I asked the right question, and he gave me the right answer. I felt it.

"Feel" is something that just *is*. It can't be taught. But it *can* be learned.

Just like cowboyin' up.

You can either cowboy up or go back and sit and wait in the truck. That's where people go who don't want to pull their weight.

Out of all those times I had to face a challenge, the most memorable was eighteen years ago when I made the decision to learn how to ride.

I was 55.

In reflecting back on the stories my mom always told me about riding, I would tell myself it sounded fun, but then, like a *lot* of things in my life, I never did anything about it.

When she died, I was determined to honor her memory and do this one thing—riding—we had talked about so many times.

My first riding experience was not very pleasant. Being a greenhorn, I didn't know what to look for in an instructor and, boy, did I make a big mistake.

After five sessions from an instructor who was more interested in watching her phone than watching me, the big old bay I was riding got spooked, and I got bucked off, landing on my right hip.

I tried to get up, but it was no use. I was stoved up pretty good.

I had fractured my pelvis in two places and spent the next twelve weeks sleeping in my leather recliner.

When I healed up, I decided to try again. A friend found me a horse and people trainer who was a real Montana cowgirl. I met her, and I liked her. She agreed to take me on as a student.

After a few lessons, she said, "I must ask you a question that's been on my mind: At your age, why did you decide to get back on and try again?"

I told her, "You know, Debbie, someday I hope the good Lord lets me see my mother again. And if I had not gotten back on a horse, the first words out of her mouth as I would be walking through the Pearly Gates would be, 'So, you got bucked off, and you didn't get back on? *Are you sure you're a son of mine?*'"

Now, I could listen to that bullshit for a day or two but *not* for *eternity*.

So, I cowboyed up, faced my fears, and I have been riding and learning the cowboy way ever since. It was my moment of truth.

Since then, I've gathered cows off the range in Idaho in sun, rain, and snow.

I've been on branding crews.

I've sorted and cut cows.

I've got a great horse, my partner and best friend Beamer.

And together, we've even won a couple buckles along the way. Not in any big event, but we worked hard to earn them.

Right now, America as a nation, and we as individual citizens, are at our *own* moment of truth.

Do we cowboy up or do we quit?

And there is no escaping this choice or putting it off, no wishing it away.

We have procrastinated long enough, and the problems have only gotten worse.

It's not just about addressing a laundry list of those problems and coming up with solutions. If it were that easy, we would have done it long ago.

It is fundamental, *foundational.*

We keep hoping that the politicians, especially the ones in Washington, will finally fix things.

There are only two things wrong with that.

First, *they* are the ones who created the mess in the first place and, second, they couldn't fix a flat tire, let alone all the problems they have created.

No, in the end it will have to be the American people who fix what ails America.

We all need to roll up our collective sleeves and clean out all the horse manure and cattle crap that has piled up for decades in this country.

From the halls of government to the executive suites at our corporations, the ivy-covered universities, Hollywood studios, and every other place in our culture and society that have been polluted and corrupted.

And this cleansing and fixing need to start at the very beginning in every home in America.

You don't need a college education or advanced degree to read and understand what I'm about to tell you in the following pages. You don't even need a high school diploma, for that matter.

All you need is common sense, a desire to pick up a manure fork, and—together with your fellow Americans—do what needs doin' and fix what needs fixin'.

Common sense is not passed down in the genes from generation to generation.

It is *taught*, passed down from parents to children.

Returning America to its former greatness and rediscovering the tried-and-true values that built this country won't be accomplished by an election.

It will only be accomplished by you and me.

It is as fundamental as being able to tell the difference between right and wrong . . . and then *acting accordingly*.

Everything else in a free society branches out from that tap root that is sunk deep into the soul of America. And while the tree of liberty that connects us all isn't healthy right now and is in danger of dying, it ain't dead *yet*.

We the people can save it if we just get back to basics.

This book is about those basics.

It's also about a fella—yours truly—who has lived many lives before, has traveled the country and the world, has been married and divorced (more than once), has had his struggles and triumphs (and struggles again . . . along with yet more triumphs) and has continued to listen, learn, and hopefully grow from all the people he's happened upon, all the adventures and misadventures he's taken on.

I like to see myself as the old guy at the end of the bar who some of the other folks in town wanna stop by and chat with.

I *don't* wanna be the belligerent and cantankerous old codger screaming at the TV down at the other end of the bar who *nobody* wants to chat with.

No, sir (and ma'am!): That ain't my style.

I aspire (and believe myself to be) the guy people pop on over to for some counsel, for some commiseration and maybe even a few laughs and, hopefully, some wisdom along the way.

The wisdom I myself have gained in large part from the last few years of working on learning to be a cowboy, and through being out with other cowboys and ranch folks—folks whose lives are about self-sufficiency and getting up early in the morning and doing all they can to take care of their land, their animals, and their families . . . often almost entirely on their own.

That's a lot of what it means to *be* a cowboy, actually. To be self-sufficient, whether home on the ranch or out on the range, strong and open to understanding what needs to be done—then doing it.

Though they can be very independent out there in the splendors of nature, they also have a strict code of ethics and values that they abide by. You really can't be a cowboy without this code. A code that I implicitly will be espousing through much of this book.

And along with that, we'll be journeying through the pages ahead in a similar circadian fashion to the cowboy himself (or herself).

I've broken this "guide to life," such that it is, into days of the week.

Being that we're talkin' cowboys here, I'm starting the week with a Monday—the first workday, since of course Sunday is a day of rest. (Though, as the old cowboy saying goes, "Work don't pay no never mind to clocks and calendars.")

Just like with the work week, as we move along from Monday through Friday, we move along, too, through our *life* that week.

Ready for what the week will be offering us and all that we have ahead, with vibrancy and passion on Monday morning. But always remembering to expect the unexpected.

Then we progress through Tuesday and Wednesday, facing new challenges, overcoming obstacles, focusing increasingly on what needs to be done throughout that week.

By Thursday and Friday, we're growing tired but also invigorated by all we've done, what we must look back on, how we've improved or adapted or evolved into a stronger and better person.

Saturday takes us toward the end, as we wrap up what we've gotta do, as we get ready to have some fun and to take on some much-deserved rest . . . which is what we find at the very end on Sunday, perhaps also with eyes to the future, to the next weeks and months and years ahead, to the next generations and to what dreams may come beyond *ourselves*.

Such is a week in the life of cowboys (and most working folk), and so too will my guide to life here be laid out. From beginning to end, Alpha to Omega, from that rising sun and rooster crow to the final dinner bell and at last tucking into bed.

Will Rogers once said, "There are three kinds of men: The one that learns by reading, the few who learn by observation, and the rest of them have to pee on the electric fence for themselves."

With this book, I hope I can do my part here—now that I'm getting to the end of my day, the end of my week—to remind my fellow mankind and particularly my fellow Americans that *it's time to stop peeing on the electric fence and then wondering why we get shocked!*

THE MEASURE OF A MAN IS WHEN
HE DOES THE RIGHT THING
EVEN WHEN NO ONE IS WATCHING.
IF YOU DO THE WRONG THING,
AND NOBODY SAW YOU DO IT,
IT IS STILL WRONG.

CSI

MONDAY

THE COMMON SENSE COWBOY'S GUIDE TO LIFE

CHILDHOOD

PETS

NOISE

EDUCATION

HUMOR

SIMPLICITY

COWBOY WISDOM

"A child's spark can become a flame and change everything. There is always one moment in childhood when the door opens and lets the future in."

—Graham Greene

CHILDHOOD

Not having kids of my own, I have to look at childhood *these* days as an observer not a participant. I *do* know that it's certainly different now from when *my* generation, the Baby Boomers, grew up. They were much simpler times when I was a boy. I can't fathom how kids can grow up now with all of these outside stimuli—cell phones and iPads, social media, TikTok, X, cineplex theaters, and a million channels on TV. Yes, *much* different from when *we* were kids.

Hold on, though: I don't want this coming off as the old "When I was your age" stuff; I'm not *attacking* the current generation. I'm more in *sympathy* here, because *our* parents and *we* as kids *didn't* have to deal with all that. Heck, back then, you maybe had three stations on the TV . . . *and you probably didn't have great reception!*

What we *did* have as kids was a lot more *freedom.* Freedom to roam around basically wherever we wanted outside and the freedom to socialize in groups by ourselves, away from adults. You could get a bunch of guys together and go down to the local ball field, choose up sides, and play a game. Baseball, football whatever. It was that easy.

You had to manage *yourselves* and deal with the pecking order. The *older* kids, usually, would act as our leaders. So, we didn't need parents there to deal with everything. We could handle and manage it all ourselves. And all we needed was some good weather, some sun, and maybe a stick and a ball.

Now, I'm also not saying here it was completely easy for *our* parents, either. But it *was* a heck of a lot different. *That's* for sure. And, although I make it sound like we were off totally on our own, the truth is that there was always some sense of eyes on us, particularly because there were a lot of stay-at-home mothers. I don't wanna say they were watching our every move, because they weren't. But they all had eyes in the back of their heads, and they all more or less looked out for each other's kids when we were at our friends' houses.

You could always walk into your buddy's house and go, "Hello, Mrs. Jones. How are you?"

"Oh, hello, Patrick! How are *you?* Would you like a sandwich? A bottle of pop?"

I think a lot of kids from my generation had similar experiences.

Kids today, though: Many have two working parents, and there are fewer stay-at-home moms. And they don't have the freedom that we had to go out and just run around and be kids (as long as you made sure to come back before dark—or, as some parents put it, "Be back before the street-lights come on").

We Boomers didn't do any favors to future generations by handing them a world that may have been a little too *adult* for them.

I also don't think we've helped ourselves or them much when it comes to how we've over-sexualized kids so early; we kinda robbed them of their innocence. We made them grow up too fast without the maturity and judgment that should go with that.

There's additionally no longer really that whole idea I was talking about before of kids in groups without adults. Oh, sure, they hang out in groups, but they have so much technology that they can share with each other. Do they learn the social skills necessary to understanding how to interact with each other and adults rather than communicating with each other screen to screen? Do they really get the chance to just be kids and learn what makes each other tick and having to understand the pecking order of the society they will soon enter and their place in it?

Back in my day, that kind of group socializing and understanding the pecking order was a precursor for what you were gonna face when you transferred from grammar school to high school. All of a sudden, you're going from your little grammar school, and you're dumped into a high school, where maybe five to ten *other* grammar schools are feeding into it. Which means you're gonna meet a whole new bunch of people, and you're gonna have to learn your place within *that* group.

Then taking the next leap, and you maybe go to *college*. In college, you found yourself once again starting at the bottom of the totem pole because you're a freshman or whatever and you had to figure things out and work yourself up the line.

Likewise, if you graduated high school and went to work right away, you had to figure that part out, too. What is your place in your new job? Likely you again start at the bottom and have to work your way up.

It's part of growing up and someday leaving childhood behind and becoming an adult.

I don't know how well kids are socialized *nowadays* because I'm not around them. I know I do see a lot of staring at phones. Sure, I'm going off of *anecdotal evidence*, but I *think* I've got a point here, if you don't mind my sayin'.

Now, I know a woman in a small town in Nebraska who works with her husband on a ranch that has been in her family for generations. She invites me every year to branding, and I haven't made it yet but someday I'm gonna surprise her.

She has two wonderful daughters. The eldest has a full schedule. She is on the speech/debate team. She also plays clarinet in the school band. She runs cross-country. She's part of the 4-H Club. She raises steers to be entered into competition at the county fair. She does all of this, *plus* her schoolwork. And if that ain't enough, she also has her ranch chores. She's a well-adjusted kid who has all these things to do. But she still gets to be a kid and has friends she can interact with and share experiences free from adults and learn from one another. Through social media, I have been privileged to watch her grow from a little girl to a young woman who will in a few years head off to college. So, I *do* know there's still kids like that out there.

But I also think we need to find more ways to let kids play and have the freedom to be kids. Let them learn the old-fashioned way: from each other.

This way, they can learn crucial lessons early, like the fact that your mom and dad aren't always gonna be there to get you out of a jam. You've got to get yourself out or, better yet, not get in a jam in the first place!

Or learning how to deal with success and failure. Kids definitely need to be supported by understanding and loving parents in those cases but supporting them doesn't mean trying to solve it for them. Sooner or later, they'll have to deal with those two things.

Better to learn early.

I don't know how much of this is gonna happen, though. Is it too late, maybe? You see all these kids they're talking about on the news who have all these problems with communication and with expressing themselves, with engaging with each other or their own family. Kids who are depressed more and more, dealing with all these problems they have or that they see in the world.

No doubt about it: childhood has changed so dramatically.

Maybe we should try to introduce some things from *before* back into childhood *today*. You know, like *not* robbing 'em of their innocence. Maybe that's wishful thinking.

Maybe the toothpaste is outta the tube, and we'll never go back; maybe that'll never happen.

But, as I keep saying, I *do* think something we Baby Boomers have to remember as we're looking at our own mortality and instead of becoming the guy at the end of the bar saying "When I was your age," (uh, oh: there it is!) that *we* have a responsibility to help bridge the differences between generations as part of our legacy. After all, we created part of this mess whether we care to admit it or not.

Back when I lived in rural California about ten years ago, there was a young boy I knew whose parents had some horses and were getting him ready to learn to ride them, too. We all rode together at the same ranch. He latched himself onto me pretty quick. He was always asking me questions, a very polite young kid. And I would chat with him every now and then, and we got along great. He was respectful and very inquisitive.

I watched him grow up over the years, as he went from a little boy who was very curious and a little bit *scared* of horses to now being out there raising his own cattle. He is a member of FFA. *(For your city folks that's Future Farmers of America!)*

It's been fun to watch him grow from the boy he was to the man he is today—check that—the actual *cowboy* he is today. And a lot of that was because of his parents and him having a passion and a purpose—something to keep him busy and learning to be a cattleman.

Now, of course, especially these days, not all kids are gonna be like that or be like the young girl in Nebraska I was talking about earlier. But I think we can *try* to help kids the way I'm talking about here, and I for one wish I could do more from where I'm standing.

But, you know, I'm a little embarrassed. I mean, *where would I start?*

One aspect of childhood I think could use some major change these days is the fact that parents aren't really being *parents* anymore. They're being *friends* and *buddies* with their kids (or, rather, *trying* to be). Well, *my* dad was *never* my friend or my buddy. He was my *dad,* and I loved him and I respected him. We *didn't* "pal around" together. What he *did* do was give me good advice until the time he died at 99 in 2017.

This idea of a more traditional parenting style goes back to earlier America. Teaching the simple truths—and the only truths really—that "right is right, wrong is wrong. If somebody needs a helping hand, you give them yours. The Golden Rule of "Do unto others as you would have them do unto you." *That* is the kind of teaching that parents should be instilling in their kids.

Too many parents today wanna make up new rules for how they're gonna raise *their* kids, without always acknowledging that—you know what?—the *old* rules were actually pretty darn good. You wonder why your kids are running doing as they dang well please? I guarantee those kids having temper tantrums in the street today for one cause or another and disrespecting authority, didn't just pick it up in high school or college. They learned it at home at a very young age.

Well, maybe parents might relearn that one simple lil' ol' word from *my* day: *"No."*

There was this one time when *I* was a kid at the grocery store with my mom, and I was nagging her for a candy bar I wanted. Kept pestering her with, "Can I have a candy bar? Can I have a candy bar? Can I have a candy bar?"

She may have been only five foot and a prayer tall, but she was tough as saddle leather. She looks right at me with those steely gray eyes of hers (so I already knew I was in some hot water here), and she says, "Patrick, that's not how to ask for something. You say, '*May* I have a candy bar? *Please*.'"

So, I say to her, "Mom, *may* I have a candy bar? *Please?*" And she says to me, "No."

Parents *used* to say no with regularity. And when they *did* say yes, there were still caveats and restrictions. "Yes, you may go to the concert tonight that's a little far away *but* make sure to be back at 11 p.m. No later or you'll be in trouble! I'm *trusting* you to be *responsible*."

These are important lessons to teach kids when they're younger, because if they don't learn to respect authority figures when they're young, they'll have to learn that lesson the *hard* way when they get older. And then *that* authority figure might very well be a *police officer*, if you catch my meaning here. *That's* when you know, and your *kid* knows, "I screwed up."

It can be very liberating: You start saying *no*, and you become a *parent* not a *buddy*.

Before I continue, I know you might say, "Well, that's easy for him to say—he never had kids!"

Understand, I know parents have a tough job, and I am not trying to tell anybody how to raise their kids.

I'm merely suggesting what used to work could work again.

Now with everything I've been talking about here, I also have to say that I *do* think its *awesome* what kids are doing today with all they've got going on, including with all the gadgets. It's like that old Groucho Marx line of, "It's so simple, a four-year-old child could understand it. Quick, get a me a four-year-old child I can't make heads or tails out of this." You get these old guys now who are saying, "God, I can't work this darn Internet thing," and they end up getting their grandson or their granddaughter to come over to help them work the newfangled thing they bought. "Oh, you do it like *this*, Grandpa," and then it's just *CLICK CLICK CLICK CLICK CLICK!* And away they go, getting it to work.

Yes, I *will* give it to the kids today that they're clearly much savvier about technology much sooner than we ever were. Maybe because we never had it! So, it's not *all* bad: It's kind of a blessing and a curse, I suppose. The blessing being that they can look up and "learn" whatever they want now as fast and as easily as a few taps or clicks. The curse being that this technology takes over so much of their lives. Is there a way that parents could help them have a little more time for some good ol' fashioned lying on the grass, looking up in the sky, and dreaming?

I wonder if *that* would help.

COWBOY WISDOM

**Money may buy a dog,
but only love will make him wag his tail.**

**Of all the things I must accept in life,
I pray silently that God will never let me
know the last time I will ride my horse.
I'd rather not know.**

PETS

I used to have a couple of Yellow Labrador Retrievers, and I loved those dogs. They were both such unique personalities. What they had in common was the fact that they both would always express that unconditional love of a dog. It's that feeling you get when they jump up on the bed and start licking you.

Nothing like it in the world.

The first dog's name was Sonny Boy. He was so even-tempered and had almost a white coat. He loved to swim in the lake near where we lived. And he shared the bed with us.

The second one, my wife (at the time) and I got during the time that my mom was dying.

Out we went to the same place where this woman had sold us Sonny Boy; we knew her pretty well, and she had another litter for us to come see.

She had this little fenced-in pen, and all the puppies were in there. My wife was talking and negotiating with the breeder to try to get the pick of the litter. Sonny Boy was the pick of his litter.

While they were jawing, I walked around the side of the pen, and this young female puppy just burst through a couple others, knocking them aside while they were holding their little paws on top of the fence. She came right up to me. It was almost like she was saying, "Pick me! Pick me!"

I'm meanwhile listening to my wife and the breeder go back and forth, "Well, no, I can't give you that one, you know, pick another one."

I just finally said, "Carol, this girl's it. This is the one." We took her home and named her Sierra Jeanne. Sierra because that is what Carol wanted and Jeanne to honor my mother and because the puppy was feisty like my mom. Carol agreed with that point!

After that, the little girl and I became very close, and she never left my side, including on the bed at night!

Now, as we all know, with both my Labs, we eventually had to do what you have to do with pets at some point when they get too old. One of the hardest things in the world, saying goodbye to a friend who's been loyal and who's loved you, and has never asked for anything other than the warmth of your house and your heart, food and just being with you.

But when it's time, you both know what must be done.

With *horses*, it's a little different. Horses aren't pets. Every horse needs a purpose. Horses need a job.

My first horse—I didn't get 'em till later in life—was Andy. Andy was eighteen, and he'd cowboyed all over the West. He'd been to Texas, he'd been up in the Dakotas, Montana, and he was a good, solid horse. After all the jobs he'd had working cows, Andy's job with me, if you will, was to teach me about horse ownership, what it *means* to own a horse.

Before Andy, I was riding and learning on *other* people's horses. We call 'em "lesson horses." They're *not* yours. You see 'em a few times a week, and you love 'em, and you take care of 'em but, again, they're *not your horse*. So, when I got Andy, here's this horse that's finally *mine*. *My* horse.

He was actually gifted to me by a father whose daughters thought they wanted to be rodeo queens—prior to their discovering boys. Out the door went being rodeo queens.

The father, he says to me, "I'm gonna gift Andy to you, 'cause you've ridden him a bunch and 'cause you want to take care of him. And as long as you give him that love, godspeed to you."

Andy taught me so much. Particularly about what you have to do to be their leader.

I didn't need to lead Andy too much, since he already knew what to do: "Okay, Patrick. Climb on, and I'll show you. I'll show you what I know. I'll teach you. Just hop on up."

Sometime later, I had *two* horses: Beamer and Andy. There was a woman taking lessons on lesson horses at the place where I kept Andy, and she had some trauma in her life. The woman's partner informed me that she thought that the horses would be good for her, because she loved riding.

So, one day I say to the woman, “Lynn, you need a horse?” She goes, “Yeah, but right now I can’t afford one. My partner and I are both on fixed incomes from retirement, from working in law enforcement.

I said, “Well, today’s your lucky day.”

And I gifted Andy to her, and she started crying.

Her partner called me later and said, “I can’t tell you how much it means to me, because Lynn really needed this at this time. It was a wonderful gift.”

I couldn’t have been happier. You pass along that special love to somebody else, and they get to experience it, too.

Paying it forward? Maybe. More like paying for today.

When I got *Beamer*, he was six. He was born on St. Patrick’s Day. (That’s right: my horse, *Patrick’s* horse, was born on St. Patrick’s Day!)

Cathi, the woman who foaled Beamer from her mare, Bunny, owned the facility where I had been keeping Andy. Her daughter, Alyssa, had been giving me lessons. Beamer is a cutting horse, and he won money when he was young. Cutting, like many Western horse events, evolved from ranch work. In this case, a horse and rider “cut” a cow out of a herd, and they must keep the cow from getting back to that herd. Cows being herd animals want to do just that. That is the basic idea. Cutting horses are very athletic and quick as cats. Beamer has great bloodlines. His grandpa was High Brow Cat, one of the greatest cutting horses of all time.

Cathi was a pro who'd won money and all kinds of awards riding cutting horses. When I decided I wanted a younger horse to challenge myself more and had decided to gift Andy once I found one, Cathi agreed to help me find my new horse.

We were looking at a bunch of different horses, and finally we were driving home one day from looking at yet another horse that we didn't like. She pulls the car over and she goes, "What the hell are we doing? We're running halfway around the country! Your next horse is sitting in my stall!"

So, we went back to her facility and put a saddle on Beamer, and I rode him for the first time, and it was just like falling in love.

He hadn't been ridden a lot during those last three years because he had been rehabbing an injury, but at this time he was sound as a dollar. And while there were certain things he had to learn and certain things that *I* had to learn, the *physical* connection was instantaneous: And over the years, that connection has developed more and more every day.

You, of course, also develop a *mental* connection with each other where, when you ride, you're feeling him underneath you. And he can feel how you are on that particular day. If you're up in your saddle and kinda tense, *he's* tense. He's a horse. He's a prey animal. He's "fight or flight." And if he feels that you're kinda unsure of yourself in the saddle, he says, "Guess what? I could run faster than you. And if a boogeyman comes out from around the corner, or a plastic bag blows in front of me, I'm dumping your ass, and I'm taking off."

However, if you're sitting deep in the saddle and you take a deep breath every now and then, and do what you can to keep yourself calm, your horse feels that. He feels, "Well, if *you're* confident, *I'm* confident."

You are the leader. And you need to earn his trust. And when you do earn his trust, it's magic. Just like true love.

Let me give you an example. A while back, after Beamer and me had moved to Utah, I was unsaddling. And the woman next to me, Megan, was unsaddling, too. She pulled her saddle off, and her saddle blanket flopped off onto the ground, and Beamer doesn't like that. So, he reacted.

Now, a couple of years ago, he might've pulled back (and backed up a *lot*), right? And been scared.

But at this moment, after years of our being together, I'm just standing there, leaning against the fence. He pops his head out and starts to move. He looks at me to see what my reaction is to the saddle blanket flopping onto the ground.

My reaction? I just look at him and I say, "Beamer, there's nothing wrong. I don't know what the hell you're doing." And he stopped. He stood there for a bit, didn't panic. He saw in me that *I* wasn't panicking. That's a connection during a situation where he's looking to you to be the leader. He's looking to you to see what you are gonna do.

If I'd grabbed the rope and yanked on him, he'd go, "Well, shit, he's grabbing me and pulling me. Something must be wrong. I better get the hell outta here!" And then I would've had a whole big problem. Instead, I just stood there talking to Megan, and Beamer calmed down. He went back to eating his grain. He trusted me. My confidence gave him confidence. *That's connection.*

The connection I have when I'm on his back, when we're sorting or cutting cows. I kind of get out of his way and, as we in the cowboy world say, "let him pick the cow." And he does! He *does* usually do it right, with the right cow. It's that trust—it's trust and connection, and our confidence in each other. And it's love. I do love him.

Yesterday, I hadn't ridden him in a couple days. So, what did I do? I sensed he didn't really want to work, and he had been in his stall with no room to run. So, I took him to the big arena, took his halter off and shooed him away. "Go run, go roll in the dirt, go be a horse." Then he bucked and rolled. I then went and did some other things. And, when he was done, he saw I was walking back towards this arena. I must have been about 40 yards from the gate. He's way over at the other end.

He pops his head up, and he takes off like a bat outta hell towards me. And I come through the gate. He's coming at me thunderously until coming to a screeching halt about, maybe, ten, fifteen yards away. I just stood there, and he walked right towards me and nuzzled me with his nose.

Does that happen every time? No. But the fact that he saw me from that far away and came running towards me was like the kinda thing you'd see with Roy Rogers and his horse Trigger. I mean, you just can't buy that kind of feeling. You can't buy that kind of loyalty.

I don't consider myself Beamer's owner. I'm his *friend.*

You might have a lot of horses throughout your life, but a lot of cowboys will tell you that there'll be one special horse that you'll always remember. For me, that's Beamer.

For a cowboy, that horse is your *partner* for work. That horse can keep you outta trouble. And you have to keep *him* out of trouble or *her* out of trouble. It's this mutually beneficial relationship. You're depending on them, and they're depending on you.

It's a bond that's hard to explain. Some people just can't understand. "What do you mean? It's just a *horse*."

But, for me, and for a *lot* of cowboys, it's the most beautiful connection I think I've ever had in my life. Maybe that's why I've had bad relationships with *humans* sometimes, because I judge them against this unique connection I have found with Beamer.

Yeah, I think my last relationship ended in part because I was spending too much time with my horse. I regret that. She deserved better from me.

Maybe what I need is a good cowgirl, because most of the ranch and cowboy people I know—the couples especially—love their critters along with each other and everything else; it's all part of one big extended family. They share a special bond. And it's beautiful to watch. Maybe, deep down, that's what I really want, too.

But for now, Beamer's my horse, and I love him, and I'm gonna take care of him. I hope he outlives me and has pastures to play in for the rest of his life. And if he *doesn't* outlive me, I'll have to face that day when it comes. But I'm ready for it either way.

That's the thing about horses and dogs. They won't be there forever. Love 'em and enjoy 'em, and what you will get in return will swell your heart every day. And it can't be explained to folks who never experience life with them.

COWBOY WISDOM

Whether you live in a crowded city or the open spaces of the country, noise or even the lack of it, is the background music of life.

Something my mother drilled into my head: "Patrick, the Good Lord gave you two ears and one mouth for a reason. Listen twice as much as you talk!" While I never forgot that I haven't always practiced it. But I can hear her say it to this day as it still rings in my two ears!

NOISE

The first thing that comes to mind is *street noise*. The sounds of cars going by or *trolley* cars, or the diesel engines of buses. That combination of horns honking, people walking on the sidewalk in a big, crowded city; maybe a siren piercing the air every now and then. Of course, that's from back when I *worked* in cities.

But when I think of my life now, the noise I hear is that of my boots as I walk onto the crunchy gravel on my way to the barn. Or the sound of all my saddle leather and metal stirrups when I throw my saddle up and it makes a noise. When I hear Beamer's hoofs on that same gravel—"Clop, clop."

Noise can also be the *rhythm* of something. The rhythm of a city daily. It's the rhythm of riding a horse. It's the rhythm of hearing your tires on the pavement as you're driving out in the country. When you're on a plane, it lands on the jetway, and you hear everybody starting to rumble, jumping out of their seats and—"click, clack"—opening all the overheads.

Noise is a part of life. And to *listen* to noises, try to identify what they are: It's kind of fun. I can't imagine *not* being able to hear the noises of life, noises of the world.

When you're in a big auditorium, just before a concert starts—the rumble of the voices, everybody's talking, and then everybody's quiet (at least at *classical* music concerts, and that sort of thing) and they're waiting for the music. Then, when it's over, they *clap*. Same kind of thing at a play.

To me, noise is so many things.

There's *human* noise combined with *mechanical* noise nowadays. It's combined with the high-tech noise of our phones buzzing on a table when somebody calls or texts you, buzzing in your pocket or buzzing on your wrist if you have an Apple Watch or similar device.

We didn't *use* to have that. That's an *intrusion*. As soon as we hear it, we go right to it: "Gosh, my phone buzzed. I better see who it is!" Well, nine times outta ten, it's probably spam.

Since we didn't *used* to have those devices. If you went and sat with somebody, had a cup of coffee with 'em, you actually had to *talk* to them, and you didn't have something interrupting your conversation. None of this, "Excuse me, I better answer that real quick." And all of a sudden, you've interrupted the *noise* of the conversation you were *having*.

What about the *inner* conversation, though? The *inner* noise in your *head*?

I think that the toughest person you have to have a conversation with is *yourself*. *That*'s the noise inside *yourself*.

And I don't mean voices in your head like you're a *nut*, like you need to be checked into a mental hospital. No, I mean the voices in your head, like, *Should I do this? Should I not do this?*

I do find, with all that noise in your head, it's much easier to talk yourself *out* of doing something than talking yourself *into* doing something.

Then there's the times when I might be going to bed, and if I don't have a clear conscience or clear mind (especially when it comes to the relationships in my life), I might start thinking, *Gosh, what did I do? How can I make it right?*

Maybe it's because a *good* thing is going on, like I'm thinking about how attracted I am to some new woman, and I can't stop hearing *her* voice in my head. Or the opposite—maybe when I'm *mad* at a girlfriend and I can't get to sleep, because I keep hearing all these *angry* voices in my head about whatever's happened, you know? That conversation that goes on in your head about what you're gonna do about it.

The biggest thing about the noises and voices in your head when it comes to this kind of thing is considering the fact that you can so often be your biggest critic. That's when you have to fight through some of the thoughts in your head. What do they say? *"You don't have to believe everything you think."*

You may be scared or worried about getting up in the morning and facing the day, facing whatever challenges that may lay ahead. As my mom used to tell me, "Get up early, and the first thing you should do is read the obituaries in the newspaper. If you're not in 'em, make coffee!"

The thing you gotta remember along with "You don't have to believe everything you think" is that *it's your voice* that's in your head. It's no one else. It's *you* communicating with *you*. Which is why you can *always* take control of the noise in your head and say to yourself, "Okay, time to cowboy up, time to go, time to *get 'er done*." All those phrases come to my mind after you make the decision to move forward. It's *your* decision. You can either give in/up and plop your butt down and not leave the couch . . . *or* you can go ride your horse and get on with the business of living.

Whatever it is, you need to just decide, "Okay, today we're gonna accomplish things. We're *not* gonna put it off until tomorrow."

And then go out and listen to the wonderful noises that there are in the world.

COWBOY WISDOM

There's no better education than adversity.

Nothin' more annoying than an educated fool. While a formal education might gain you some knowledge, only life experiences will gain you wisdom. A PhD won't help you fix a flat tire.

EDUCATION

One time, I was working with Beamer, and Trudy's son Paul was trying to help me learn to master some exercises to make us both better at working cows.

Paul quoted me a famous trainer who said, "When you're working with your horse, you gotta make the *right* things *easy* and the *wrong* things *difficult*." That's because, when you're working with your horse, what you're *really* doing is asking him a question. You wanna get the right answer, the right response to your leg and hand cues.

If you get the wrong answer, the wrong response . . . well, maybe you're asking the wrong question of him. "Why isn't he doing what I want him to do?" It's because you need to do a better job of how you're asking the question or maybe even the question *itself*, as I just said.

I have to keep reminding myself of this.

That's a lot of what education is about, I think. Asking the right questions. Understanding how to communicate what it is you want, how to best learn what it is you want to know in the most effective way.

You can't learn unless you ask questions.

Education was *paramount* to my mom and my dad. Absolutely paramount.

My brothers and I were all born in San Francisco. There we were, living in the city, and to quote Mark Twain (or at least it's attributed to him), "The coldest winter I ever spent was the summer I spent in San Francisco." There's a lot of fog in the mornings, and my mom got tired of putting coats on kids (even in July!) to go out and play. So, we moved to Marin County across the Golden Gate Bridge, which meant my dad would have to then commute (no big deal to him).

Marin at that time was still kind of semi-rural, post-World War II. There were still dairies in the northern and western part of the county. It was nothing like the swanky, upscale place it has become today. It had two high schools when we got there, and by the time I'd grown up, there were *six*. Just to show you how fast the place grew from what had basically been a bedroom community for wealthy San Franciscans in the summertime (since the weather was warmer there than in the city).

At first, we were living in a small house in one area, and we went from a family of six to one of seven when my sister was born. Things got crowded in that little house, and my parents were looking for something bigger.

But my parents wanted to move to a place with the best school. After doing her homework, my mom wanted us to move to a *different* town there called Ross. Where there were a lot of *big*, opulent houses.

My mom was always very positive and hopeful, and even though my dad wasn't sure if we could afford to move to Ross, my mom would just smile and say, "We're gonna do it!" Mom was our rock.

And you know what? She *did* find a house in Ross. A run-down, big piece of property.

She had a vision. She always wanted a big yard for her kids. That's what this house had. Still, her vision was a bit different than my dad who was concerned we were going to be stretched financially. That was when mom found out that the real estate agent guy was . . . "fond of his liquor." So, she made sure that he was liquored up when she made the deal. That's how we got the place!

There was our big backyard—a *jungle*. My mom basically hacked her way through it. With the help of some tree experts, she handled most of it herself.

All of this because she wanted us to live where we kids could go to one of the best schools in the county. My mom wanted us to have the *best* possible education. My siblings and I ended up going to that school, and it *was* idyllic in terms of all the great teachers we had there. We were so lucky.

I still remember the joy of learning there. Our great teachers opened up so many doors for us. And we didn't have the distractions of today, without all of today's technology, which can sometimes be helpful for learning but can also stand in the way of learning how to do certain things yourself. Call me "wistful" if you need to, but I still think you need to *learn your way through the world*. You can't Google your way through.

Ross Grammar School was great. I loved it. I absolutely loved it. We had teachers like Mr. Brunkenhoefer, who was originally from Texas, complete with the accent.

Mr. B, as we called him, commanded respect. He believed in discipline but was still approachable.

He didn't approve of boys walking around with our shirt tails hanging out, which was a style in those days. Looks like today it's returned. Mr B. thought it was sloppy and slovenly for young men, and if he caught you like that, he made you tuck in your shirt. That's not all, either! He'd also make you write a penance and have it on his desk bright and early the next morning. A couple years ago, I ran into an old friend of mine at a memorial service for three of our buddies from school, and we looked at each other and laughed as we recited the line to each other completely:

HENCEFORTH AND FOREVERMORE, I SHALL SHUDDER AND QUAKE AT THE MERE THOUGHT OF CAVORTING ABOUT IN THE SIMIAN STYLE WITH MY SHIRT TAILS FLAPPING GAYLY IN THE BREEZE.

You had to write that one hundred times. And penmanship counted!

That was back in the day, when teachers knew they had the support of the parents. The teachers knew they could discipline us kids how they saw fit. And I don't mean abuse. I mean good, old-fashioned *discipline*. It was the parents' job to send kids to school prepared to learn, and it was the teachers' job to *teach.*

In sixth grade, we had a teacher—Mrs. Moran—who would read to us for about a half hour or so after lunch, kind of to help us settle down from being out and running around on the playground like "wild Indians," as they used to say.

One of these books she read us that I'll surely never forget was called *Little Britches*. It was a story about a young boy growing up in the West who had the nickname of (you guessed it!) "Little Britches." A beautiful story written by a guy named Ralph Moody. He wrote a *few* books. But we really loved this particular *book* that allowed us to fantasize about being like the boy in it, running around barefoot and riding a horse bareback, wearing a pair of bib overalls, and all the rest of it. Kinda like Tom Sawyer.

Then, one day after lunch, we came in, and Ms. Moran had a special guest waiting for us. It was Ralph Moody, the author! So, we got a chance to hear from and speak with him. Amazing!

By the time I got to high school, I played freshman football, mainly because my *brothers* played, and they were all good football players.

We started out a group of boys, some who you knew and some you didn't. I weighed about 110 pounds dripping wet, and I was on the third string. We had a great coach who took this bunch of strangers and molded them into a team. Everybody pulled for each other and by the end of the season we were 4-3. We'd had a winning season. I'll never forget those guys.

It was a molding experience for me personally, something that has stuck with me after all these years. In fact, when I went to my 50th high school reunion, I walked up to an old friend, and I said, "66!" and he said, "33!," 'cause he was number 66, and I was 33. So, again, my experience playing football, *that* was part of my education in becoming who I am today, too.

Sports at a young age are important and an important part of your larger education, I believe, because you're developing new friendships, you're having to learn how to be part of a team and realize your role on that team. It's like a microcosm for the larger society outside of your team, outside the field, outside the game.

By the end of those four years of school and playing sports, your teammates and you become a solid group. Often, that's true for your class, too, which is why I'm still in touch with a lot of the people (who are still around!) who I graduated with.

But, for me, when I look back on my formal education in school, I do keep reflecting on how fortunate we were. Fortunate to have such good teachers. Fortunate that my siblings and I had a mother and father who took our education so seriously and sacrificed so much for us. My mom, though, wow: She really watched over my siblings' and my grades *like a hawk!* She made sure we were doing everything we were supposed to be doing in school—and *then* some! My dad was brilliant, and he oversaw the whole operation, but he never could quite get me to understand math or how to use the slide rule, no matter how hard he tried.

Another thing I'll tell you about my mom: When I was a *sophomore* in high school, I was feeling my oats pretty good and was hanging out a bit too much with the older kids, partying a little too much. What had to happen happened, and my grades suffered.

My dad was threatening to send me to military school. He said, "You need *discipline*, Patrick!" But, my mom? She was telling my dad *not* to send me to military school, because, as she put it, "Patrick will figure out a way to *like* it there!" So, instead, she told my dad to make me *stay* where I was but to make me *work*. *Really* work in my studies and my time at school.

And that's what they did: They did make me *work*.

By the time I was a *junior*, all of a sudden—boom! I was rebuilding myself—something I would have to do many times in my life. Which led to, by the time I was a senior, my doing *great*.

That was good, but, unfortunately, that bad sophomore year probably kept me out of a couple of universities that my folks wanted me to go to. So, *that* was something of a lesson, something of an *education* for me, too.

It made me realize I needed to carve out my *own* life.

Actually, you could say that was the beginning of my heading a separate way. Then, I tell you what: I really didn't know where I was heading at the time, especially since I was going off on my own. I didn't know what I wanted to do.

I ended up working a job, saved some money, and, in the summer of '71, went to Europe, and I stayed for *six months*. And you better believe *that* was *another* kind of education for me. You bet!

I ended up working in youth hostels in England, and there I met a great guy—a Church of England priest Father Barnaby—and one day he says to me that they were closing down the hostel where I was working. "So, what are you going to do next?" I said I didn't know. I asked him if he had anything else for me to do so that I could stick around.

Then he goes, "Patrick, you're a very smart guy. I think you should *go home*." He tells me I should go back to school to find out where I belonged in the world. He continues that he'd *love* to have me around still but that it was time for me to move on, to continue my education.

I took his advice, I went home, and that's when I said to myself, "Okay, time to buckle down, time to throw away the wanderlust—at least for now!" And I went back to school to a junior college. And you know what? I got myself *great* grades. I did so well there, I was able to go where a buddy of mine was going to school at the University of Oregon. Once *there*, I got myself straight A's.

In fact, to make up for lost time with all my screwing around, I went straight through, including summer school. Which allowed me to graduate only two quarters late from where I should have if I had gone right out of high school.

My parents came up to see me graduate, and they were so proud of me. They weren't just proud I'd graduated from college, but that I had done it *in my own way*. It was especially powerful to see that in my dad, because we had definitely come to loggerheads a few times when I was younger, and I knew he had lost a little faith in me from time to time, but my mother wouldn't let that happen.

To see my dad there at my college graduation, to see him realizing, "God damn it, Patrick did it!" was always a great source of pride for me. Especially after having gone my own way to get there. And I know my dad was very proud of me.

My formal education ended that day in March 1975.

My life education had just begun.

COWBOY WISDOM

It's better to grow old with a sense of humor, than to grow old with no sense at all.

Learn what's important and what's not. And what's on TV usually isn't. Unless it's about cowboys, cowgirls and horses. *That's* important!

HUMOR

There's a great cowboy line that says, "*Anybody* can learn how to cowboy, but it takes a damn *genius* to make any money at it." Makes you realize you have to keep a sense of humor in everything you're doing. Gotta have a good time while you're at it. We're talking here about a certain *outlook*.

An outlook like this is what Will Rogers had. Mark Twain, too. Even when times were tough, they'd poke fun at a lot of things, including some of the big wigs. Which would give everyday people the thought that there was someone out there pitching for them.

Will Rogers, Mark Twain, and humor like they wrote and spoke about help people remember that we shouldn't take things too seriously in this country. I think we've lost some of that perspective, and we need to get back to it, since now we're at a time when people get so mad and so "offended" at some of the humor out there, which is a real shame.

Now, a guy getting up on stage and just shouting, "Fuck you! Fuck you! Fuck you!" the whole time is *not* humor. It's not very original and not insightful. Jerry Seinfeld was popular as a standup comic because he would talk about everyday things, just like Mark Twain, and Will Rogers. Jerry did it in a funny way without having to use all these cuss words the whole time.

Most of the cowboys I've met are pretty funny, too. They have a good time making fun of situations when things go wrong. "Anything that doesn't kill you . . . is *funny*," they'll say. Somebody gets bucked off a horse and, as long as he gets up and he's okay, it can become funny. It can create a whole story of how it happened. It's not laughing at the person, it's making light of something to release the tension in a situation where if he didn't get up it could be a very different result, I think.

Then that becomes a great story around the campfire after the day's work is done. And the story grows hair—before you know it, the story becomes one of the guy getting bucked off a horse that was ten feet tall, and the horse was snorting fire out of its nose and out its ass! "The poor guy went sailing, and he turned around in mid-air, came back down and landed right in the saddle." The story becomes *cartoonish* and *funny*. I'm kidding, of course, but not by much!

When things get tough, that's when you should start *laughing and keep your sense of humor*; at least you're gonna have fun while you're trying to get *out* of that tough spot.

I actually have personal experience of one of those "cowboy has a wreck and it's funny" stories. My friend and Idaho rancher Jen called me and said, "Hey, the weather finally cleared, and we're gonna be branding next weekend. Come on up." I had been to three fall gatherings and another branding with her and her family previously and had a wonderful time. They are salt-of-the-earth people.

So, we gathered up the cows, and the branding was about to commence.

The calves were sorted out from their mamas and put in a corral, which we'd all helped construct from fence panels that had been brought on a flatbed truck. The cowboys go in and they rope the calves at the hind legs. They drag them to the fire; the calves are held down, and one person vaccinates them with their big vaccine gun, and then somebody else has got the branding iron and gets the deed done. And there is also castration for the males.

While *this* is going on, the mama cows are being held back outside the corral, 'cause they want their babies. You *took* their babies, and they want them back!

There's this one calf that's getting pulled out, and it's big enough that it stepped out of his rope loop and started charging towards us in the branding pit. I had my back to him, because I was the one doing the vaccinations, and I turned around and looked and, as I looked, *it was right on top of me*.

I'm knocked down, and it's running right up my chest. I'm trying to grab it, and, all of a sudden, as I'm rolling around with it on the ground, I look up again, and now the *mama* is bearing down on me! She's coming to get her baby calf! It's like, "Oh, *crap*!"

I don't remember if I prayed or what, but, really, there was nothing I could do at that moment—*the mama cow was COMING!* And then all I saw were the legs of a horse and the leg of a cowboy, boot in the stirrup. Martin, the awesome Mexican cowboy had charged up and got between me and that angry mama cow, and he stopped her from running me over, and everybody's real quiet for a second.

I got up and started dusting myself off, spitting dirt outta my mouth. Then everybody started laughing. (They're, of course, also asking if I'm okay and all that.)

Because I was still new to all of this, at first I thought they were making fun of me. I thought they were laughing *at* me. But it was another lesson I learned out there on the range: They *weren't* making fun of me. After all, they had all gone through similar things. It's part of the cowboy way out there. These things do happen. And they happen to *everyone*.

One of the cowboys even pulled me aside and told me as much. It wasn't that they were laughing at *me*, but rather at the *situation*. It was more like *nervous* laughter, because it's something everyone's gone through at one time or another.

It's an important lesson: Everybody's been through stuff, so don't laugh *at* 'em; laugh *with* 'em. Because "there but for the grace of God go I" (or *we*) at *some* point in your life.

Humor, comedy: a lot of it is also about *relatability*. It's about *commiseration, connecting* with each other, even people that you might not get along with very well.

I think that *standup* comedy in particular is very good for this. And people like Will Rogers, who would just "tell it like it is." It's through comedy like Will's and what we see with some of the best standup comedy that we discover these all-too-important "peeks" into our culture, that we see we're part of a larger whole, of *America*. Different *slices* of America, but nonetheless America as a whole. It's in this way that humor and comedy can remind us that, whatever differences we all have, we're still *all* Americans.

At the same time, as I've said before, I really think people need to take humor and comedy less seriously, less *personally*.

I was watching an old episode of *Seinfeld* the other day, and he made a gay joke that was pretty funny and pretty harmless. Nevertheless, it was definitely one of those moments where I said, "Gee, if he made that joke *today*. . . . Yeah, there's no way." To which I would just tell people, again, *don't take yourselves so damn seriously*.

I don't know who started this damn thing of telling everyone what they *can* say and *not* say, what they *can* joke about and *not* joke about. But, I tell you something: I think all it *really* does is *divide the country*.

Humor and comedy *can* bring us all together as Americans. So, going *against* that and telling everyone *else* what to say and what is and isn't permitted to be joked about . . . well, that's *not* America. Ironically, it's the kind of thing that happens in the countries that tend to be our enemies.

It's my hope that we can get back to the point where we can laugh at each other and have funny movies that bring us back together again. *Caddyshack* was a great movie. I think *Planes, Trains and Automobiles* is one of the best movies I've ever seen, because there's comedy, but there's also *pathos* in it. It's a John Hughes movie, and he's always got a little message in there along with the humor.

I think that's important, because you'll be splitting your sides over the jokes and, at the same time, you'll also be getting something *else* out of it. You have John Candy's character running around and selling shower curtain rings. You can tell he's a pretty sad guy, and, yet, what does he keep through it all? His sense of humor. When things get bad, he tries to laugh at the situation rather than let it get him down.

Then there's Steve Martin's character, who's the model of straight-ass society, a society that can't be bothered by working-class guys like Candy's character.

Both characters are trying to get home for the holidays, and along the way, they start getting better at understanding one another. And a lot of that happens through the humor they can find and share a belly laugh or two.

I do believe we would find this kind of understanding amongst each other, too, nowadays if we laughed more—not necessarily laughing *at* other people or *swearing* every five seconds—but the kind of laughter that would really bring us together the way Steve Martin's and John Candy's characters in *Planes, Trains and Automobiles* find a way to come together through sharing laughter when things get their worst—as they do in the film!

I really think this is vital to America. And I do hope we can get back to that.

COWBOY WISDOM

If you don't have much to say, don't take an hour to prove it.

It's the simplicity of country life that heals the soul. No rush. No noise. Just you and the world as it's meant to be.

SIMPLICITY

I've sometimes been around these politicians who talk in circles—they talk, and talk and talk . . . but never say *anything*. When all you *really* want them to do is give you a simple answer or simple solution.

It's almost as though they think that the more words they throw out there, the smarter they sound. When, in actuality, they sound pretty stupid, because most people wanna be spoken to *directly* and, yeah, in a simple way. You know: "Tell me what you wanna tell me. Don't use a lot of ten dollar words to tell me your thoughts that ain't worth a penny. No fancy words. Tell it to me straight. I can take it. I'm an *adult*."

Then there's the kind of simplicity a lot of us crave in getting away from the *rush* of life everywhere, especially in big cities and suburbs. "We gotta do this, we gotta do that. The kids have soccer practice. We have that trip planned."

I understand: It's part of our society today. But there are ways of bringing simplicity even to a more harried "modern" lifestyle. Instead of planning some huge, complicated overseas vacation, why not keep it simple and go on a road trip. Visit a national park. See America. Stay in motels. Take away the kids' phones. Put yours away, too! And then you and the kids can talk on the way to your destination. You can have a real family conversation instead of everyone being on their phones the whole time.

I guess it's okay that so many people are rushing around these days, and schedules are crammed beyond belief and that America overall has gotten as complex as it is. But in this rush, what are we missing out on? What about letting kids just see the beauty of nature? What about our kids having the solitude of thinking by themselves, instead of being pushed so hard that they can't be kids? If we could have kids whose lives weren't so complex and who could get to enjoy the simplicity of life, it would probably be better for their growth into adulthood, their overall mental health as well as that of society as a *whole*.

I think it's possible that can happen, because *each generation rebels against the past ones*. And I think these new generations that have had their lives filled with all kinds of stuff so early on might soon enough decide that they want to go a different direction.

I think they'll at least be open to it. They might say, "Gosh, that was a lot of pressure on *me*, and things were so *complex* when *I* was growing up. I want *my* kids to have some *freedom*. I want *my* kids to learn stuff on their own. I want *my* kids to live a simpler life."

I have no empirical evidence to back it up. I just think that there's gonna be a reaction to all this.

And I *do* think we got *way* too much shit going on. People gotta slow down a little bit.

We do *that*, and we'll find that it's gonna be better for every generation to come, that everybody needs to just take some time and take a deep breath. I'm not the one who came up with it, but I think we should all subscribe to the maxim of, *"When you're going through life, save a little time for dreaming and for breathing."*

(And just to *keep* it simple, I think we'll end this segment a bit early!)

YOUR WORD IS YOUR BOND,
AND YOUR HANDSHAKE SEALS THE DEAL.

TUESDAY

THE COMMON SENSE COWBOY'S GUIDE TO LIFE

FRIENDSHIP

BULLYING

INDIVIDUALITY

REBELLION

IDEALISM

LOVE

COWBOY WISDOM

A good friend knows all your stories.
A best friend lived them with you.

FRIENDSHIP

You ready for *this* one? Here it is: To be a good friend, you know . . . *be a good friend.*

And that means *first* be a good friend to *yourself*. Self-love. You gotta like yourself *first* if you expect anybody *else* to like you. Along with that, be the kind of person people will *want* to be friends with and treat others with *respect*. As John Wayne said, "Treat everybody with respect until they give you a reason *not* to." Pretty simple, huh?

But what does it *mean* to be a good friend? Or a friend at all?

We say all the time things like, "That guy's my friend" or even "That person's my *best* friend." Younger women have shortened it to BFF (best friends forever) or "bestie." But however *you* talk about it, whatever you call it, a "long-lasting friendship" means that you've *gone through something, a shared experience* with that person you're a long-term friend of.

I was fortunate enough to grow up in a place that was kind of magical. You wouldn't think Marin County in Northern California *today*—one of the richest counties in America—was the same place as it was when I was growing up there. No! It wasn't like that back then. It was simpler, *Wonder Years* style.

There were a lot of large families. And when I say *large*, I mean three to five kids in a lot of cases. Darn few single-child families. With a lot of generational connections—your older brother would always know an older brother of someone *else* you knew. Your sister would be in the same class as someone *else's* sister you knew. That kind of thing. It was all very intimate.

Which meant, too, that the guys I grew up with, I'm still friends with today. We've lost three of them in the last couple of years. It's especially hard, because this is the time in a man's life when you've moved past *parents* dying and now it's *contemporaries* dying, which in turn makes it feel like death is looking you right in the eye. Makes you realize more than ever that there's a limit to this life.

But back when we were all growing up together, we could go up to the lakes and reservoirs in the area and spend hours and hours catching lizards, running around getting dirty all day and playing "Cowboys and Indians" or "Army" or whatever. It was an idyllic place to grow up in and really bonded us all together for life.

Then again, in college I made some friends who are still friends of mine, too.

That helped grow and expand my childhood group of friends, because a lot of us who grew up where we did in

Northern California ended up going to the (relatively) nearby University of Oregon in Eugene together. I was pretty fortunate to have that kind of friend base, a base that started when I was young and grew and grew through college.

I must be honest and say I have been remiss over the last years about staying in contact. Life got in my way, but still no excuse.

After college, you start making *other* friends—people you work with, people you meet elsewhere along the way. And then you get older still, and that's when it can become harder to make new friends—especially male friends—with whom you have a deep, deep connection.

Yeah, you'll make friends *throughout* your life. *No question about it*. But the ones you really make that connection with, the ones that really last are those who you've gone through something with. Friends who, when something happens to *them*, hit *you* personally.

We had a memorial service for three members of the gang I grew up with about a year ago, and I got to see a lot of the old gang there. These were the guys I went to kindergarten with, I went to high school with, and, in some cases, went to college with. We had learned about girls together, we had learned about a *lot* of things together.

These are the kinds of friendships that last. Growing up together, getting dirty and in trouble together, learning together . . . and now meeting up again later on in life at memorials, and reunions and that sort of thing together. If you're lucky like me, those friendships can last your whole life.

I've definitely made some other friends more recently as I've gotten older. People like my horse trainer Trudy and her son Paul. People like the guy who's my blacksmith, my farrier. It's a different kind of friendship, because these aren't the same kind of friends I grew up with. One of the many things I've learned with these new friends is that, if you're lucky too, every friend you make can be a learning experience. You can learn about who these new friends are, learn about their lives and learn about how they got to where they are.

And that's pretty special, since a lot of the time, of course, and as I mentioned, as you get older and older, it can be harder and harder to make new friends. *Good* friends.

So, whenever you *do* have the chance to make new friends—do it. You can never have too many friends.

For me, I've done so much crap all over the country that I've been fortunate enough to meet people from different walks of life, become friends with them, learn from them and sometimes be able to trust *them* and have them trust *me*.

And that's, again, one of the most important things, too. A good friend is somebody you can *trust* (I would say with your *life*). Somebody where you can say to yourself, "If I'm in trouble, I can trust that person." And trust, I've always said, is like virginity: If you ever lose it, you're never gonna get it back again.

When it comes to the cowboy way, friends and *trusting* your friends are so important, because you *are* quite literally trusting these people with your life, particularly when you're out there on the range or getting into what can often be dangerous situations.

Take those more recent friends of mine—Trudy, her son Paul and her husband Skip. They're teaching me skills I've never known or used before. I'd ridden horses before I met them, but we're still talking here about sitting on top of, and trying to control, a 1,200- to 1,500-pound animal that could kill you if you're not careful and don't know what you're doing.

So, I have to really trust what Trudy, Paul and Skip are telling me, are teaching me, because they've grown up in this world, and I haven't. I have to trust them as they teach me their way of life—the cowboy way. A lot of what is "old hat" for them is still very new for me. I have to trust them, because they're my friends. And, in a lot of ways, they're my friends because I (can) trust them.

Putting your life in someone else's hands does create that feeling of kinship with them.

One time, Trudy and I were working with Beamer in a big indoor arena out in Bellevue, Idaho, near where I was living. It was toward the end of wintertime, just before spring. That's when the ice and the snow on top of the buildings starts to melt and can (and *does*) slide off the roofs of those buildings. We're in this arena whose sides are made of sheet metal, and when the snow slides off and bangs into the walls, it can sound like a *cannon* going off. And it echoes! You can only imagine what happened when this was going on and Beamer and I were riding around inside the arena.

Luckily, Trudy taught me what to do if he spooks. I knew everything to do, thanks to Trudy and her tutelage.

But this was one case when Beamer got spooked, and I just didn't have time to react to it properly. When the snow came off the side of the building and hit the wall, it sounded like a howitzer, Beamer got spooked, broke to one side and I got pitched off.

I hit the ground and I hit the ground *hard*. I'm trying to get up, and Trudy comes over with her calming voice: "Lie down on your stomach, don't get up. You got the wind knocked out of you, so *just lie down*."

Trudy's soothing voice and everything she was saying immediately calmed me down from the fall.

If you've never experienced that kind of thing before, no matter how long you've ridden, you get *scared* when you fall like that, because you wanna know, "Do my legs work? Do my hands work? Do my arms work? Did I break something? Is my head gashed open?"

I was fine or at least *thought* I was fine. So, I thought I'd get back up on Beamer. But Trudy kept me off. She told me, "*No.*" She told me that the snow was still falling and that Beamer may get scared again and that the next time, I could fall and really hurt myself. And let's not put you both through that twice in one day.

Here was my friend. My friend Trudy. Who I trusted. Who had earned my trust. Who had my life in her hands. And, so, I did what she said. I trusted her over my own judgment in that moment. That right there is friendship.

In fact, there was another time a little after that when we were outdoors on an obstacle course. Beamer got spooked and pitched me again. It was my fault, not his. But this time, Trudy said I *should* get back on him. So, I did. And

Beamer was fine, and I was fine on the rest of the obstacle course.

This isn't, I should point out, Trudy "babying" me. It's just a matter of the fact that she's the expert here, she's been doing this her whole life and, as a longtime friend now, I trust her to the point that when she tells me to stay off Beamer, I stay off. When she tells me I can get back on him, I get back on him.

That's the kind of friendship, the kind of *connection* I have with Trudy.

This is all why a lot of the cowboy world is built on trust. You gotta work together with the people you're riding with.

Every time you get on a new crew, you've just *gotta* all trust each other, *trust* that you know what you're doing and that you're gonna protect each other. Not everyone's gonna become your longtime friend, but when you're all out there together, that trust does *need* to be there, and that means, ideally, you can share some real friendship at that time, at least.

Whether it's childhood friends, whether it's friends I've made later in life, whether it's friends in the cowboy world, for me, it's all about the basic thing of giving your trust to somebody and their reciprocally trusting *you* in return.

That's what makes a true friend.

COWBOY WISDOM

"No man in the wrong can stand up against a fellow that's in the right and keep on a-comin'."

—Motto of the Texas Rangers

Bullies are by nature cowards.

BULLYING

There's an old cowboy saying: "You're better to shoot your rifle by mistake than your mouth on purpose."

Words are just as powerful as fists sometimes, and you can get yourself into a whole heap of trouble if you're not watching what you're doing *or* saying. But you know what? A lot of that is on *you*.

If you're a kid literally doing nothing but riding your bike down the street and you get jumped by some bigger kids looking for a fight for no reason, that's a different story than riding your bike past those kids and shooting your mouth off without any provocation. If you get beat up in *that* case, well . . . maybe you had to pay a consequence for *your* actions, if you know what I mean. That's an overall life lesson, especially for young boys: *Life has consequences*.

You see it all the time in sports stadiums now: guys wearing football jerseys, drunker than shit, getting in fights. Over *what?* Yeah—probably got too much booze in 'em!

I remember what my mom taught us boys (there were *four* of us), and one of the things she said was, "If I ever catch you starting a fight for no reason, you're in trouble. *But*, if I catch you walking away from one where you're getting picked on, you're in trouble, too."

She also said that, "If somebody is in trouble, and I catch you walking away when you could help, *you're in trouble*."

I think her whole point was—and it's in all the cowboy codes I follow even today—you gotta defend the weak, the people getting preyed upon. That's part of the responsibility of being a man. Standing up for those who can't stand up for themselves or who are overpowered. At the same time, though, my mom didn't mean that every time you get challenged, it should automatically turn into a fight.

No. What she meant was: There are times when you're not gonna have any option but to stand and fight, and that's, quite frankly, part of being an *American*, too. That's part of the *American spirit*. This is all, too, part of the cowboy way, as I said earlier.

But I will tell you something: Nobody likes a bully.

Nobody likes a loudmouth, and nobody likes somebody who's going around picking fights. Especially if you're out in the cowboy world, and you got work to do, you're herding cows, or you're branding cows or you're building fences, whatever it is, whatever the job is that you're doing—nobody needs somebody around who thinks they're a big shot and goes pushing people around. In fact, if there *is* someone around like that, eventually the group's gonna take care of it.

Now, yes, if somebody's being set upon by a couple of people, and you see it, I say step in and stop it. Unfortunately, nowadays you see videos all the time on YouTube of adults standing by when kids are wailing on each other. Or worse, they're encouraging and filming themselves. You're an adult! Stop what's going on! That's part of being an adult!

We're all gonna have to learn sooner or later in life, whether you've got a bully on the playground in school, or you got a bully in the workplace who's pushing folks around, at some point you gotta stand up and be counted. At some point, you gotta stand up on your own hind legs and say, "That's enough, and I'm not gonna tolerate this anymore!"

When I was younger, after I got outta college, my brother Rob and I played in the San Francisco Rugby Club together. I played in college at the U of O, and Rob took it up later. There was this one guy on a particular team we had played before who had it in for me. I don't know why. We're playing a match, and all at once, out of nowhere, this guy I'm talking about comes up to my side. He says, "Hey!" I turn and he hits me so hard in the temple that he just *flattens* me onto the ground.

I went down face first, and my brother Rob was right behind me. He saw the whole thing. He saw that it was totally unprovoked. Our coach at the time was a doctor at the UCSF Medical Center. That day, he wore a white windbreaker. He had long salt-and-pepper hair and a long beard to match.

So, he came over to me to see if I'm okay. He leaned over me, and the sun was directly behind him. I look up at him, and because of his long beard and long white hair, all I could think was, "Oh, God. It's Jesus Christ, and I'm *dead!*" That's how woozy I was by this guy who had come up out of nowhere and pummeled me in the temple.

Anyhow, my brother sought the guy out and he said, "Hey, that guy you hit was my brother."

The guy goes, "Yeah, so what?"

And my brother hit him so hard that he broke the guy's nose.

But you know what? That was the only time he ever defended me like that. Why? Because when we were boys, he told me that he would always be there to help me and stand by me. But he would not fight my battles for me. I'd have to stand up and fight my own battles. He would only ensure that if it came to a fight, he would make sure it was a fair one. "I'm not always gonna be there, Patrick, and you're gonna have to take care of yourself."

I think this one time, he knew I was too groggy to do anything about it so he decided he'd take care of it for me.

It's something that parents sometimes have to say to strengthen their young boys especially. You gotta tell 'em, "I'm not always gonna be there, and you're gonna have to fight your way through life sometimes."

These days, though, we've got too many young men who think their strength comes from the bottom of a can instead of through character. Character is so vital to becoming a real adult, to becoming a man. You must have a code in your life. What do you measure your decisions in life against? Do you have a code? What is your moral background? What is your ethical background that makes you be who you are?

You gotta figure that out for yourself so that, instead of just doing something because everybody else is doing it, you can say, "I can't do that, 'cause that's against my code."

COWBOY WISDOM

You can't weigh the facts if you've got the scales loaded down with your opinion.

Just because you're following a well-marked trail, doesn't necessarily mean whoever broke it knew where the heck they were going. I'll bet the Donner Party wished they had heeded this advice.

INDIVIDUALITY

If you don't have individuality, you're just a worker bee in the hive; you're just a drone, and you're just a follower.

Now, is that such a bad thing? Not necessarily, actually. Because, after all, the world *does* need drones.

Beyond this superficial idea of what individuality is, though, is the concept that it has to do with your own inner strength. It has to do with who you are as a person. And in *that* case, you don't *have* to be a star.

Take my horse trainer Trudy, for one. Now, *she's* an individual. A truly unique person. We all have our *own* uniqueness, but Trudy grew up as a young girl and then a young lady who was expected to pull her own weight on the family ranch. Gender didn't matter.

This sort of upbringing is true for a *lot* of people in rural areas, especially farms and ranches, because, well . . . children, as soon as they're able, are another set of hands to do work.

And, so, Trudy was expected to do everything that the boys did, that her brothers did. This meant that even when she was learning how to rope, she was competing *not* in a "girl's division" but against boys and, later in life, men. This greatly helped Trudy forge an inner strength and—absolutely—her own sense of individuality. *Remember that Ginger Rogers danced every step Fred Astaire did, but she had to do it backwards and while wearing high heels!*

My mom was like that—expected to pull her own weight regardless of gender, size, age, whatever. This is something that is instilled into you by your parents, but you've gotta, in the end, *develop* it *yourself*. We all have to mold ourselves through each of our *individual* life experiences.

To be clear, although I know a lot of people think that, for life experience to have any real impact, it needs to be *dramatic*. Which is *not* true. When you learn to tie your shoe as a young kid, *that's* a real accomplishment, and it's some real-life experience that can help shape who you are later down the road. It helps you learn, at a young age, how to do things for yourself.

When I was growing up, there was a kid who was a dear and close friend. I remember that once as a young boy I was invited to have dinner at his house, and his mom would cut his meat for him. She asked me if I wanted her to cut mine and I said, "No ma'am." I already knew how.

When my friend came over for dinner at *my* house, meanwhile, well . . . it was *every man for himself!*

My friend was just sat there when my mom brought the plates of food in for everyone from the kitchen. He sat there next to my mom like he had no idea what to do (because he *didn't*). It wasn't his fault he hadn't learned how. And my mom looked at my dad, and my dad looked at me. I shrugged.

Mom finally said to my friend, "Mike, you gonna cut your meat?" And *he* said, "I don't know how."

My mom (and the rest of my family) being who she is, she (and none of the rest of us) made fun of Mike or anything. (If any of us Dorinson boys had done *that*, we would've gotten the back of Mom's hand for our indiscretion!) No, *instead* Mom gently told Mike to pick up his knife and fork, and she'd teach him. And that is exactly what she did.

And you never seen a kid so happy in your whole life over something as simple as cutting his own meat!

The *next* time I went to Mike's house for dinner, his mother brought out his plate of food, and she started to cut his meat. (Mike's father *hated* that she did that, I should add. He just didn't say anything about it.) Anyway, Mike told his mom right then, "I can cut my own meat." And his mom was *shocked*.

Mike's dad asked, "Who taught you?"

"Mrs. Dorinson taught me," Mike answered. And his father had the biggest smile you ever saw.

Now, cutting your own meat might be a small thing, but, like tying your shoes yourself for the first time, it helps shape who you are. *Anything* you do for yourself at a young age helps you to become the person, the *individual* you become later on in life, because you learn how to depend on *yourself* and you learn how to do things and live life in your own individual way.

Nowadays, we've got *machines* that do a lot of stuff for us. We've got phones that think for us. As somebody once told me, *Google probably knows more about you than you do*. But you know what? If your tire blows out, and you're out in the middle of nowhere (like where I was last week!), there's nobody around, and there's no cell service—you're gonna have to fix the tire *yourself*. Otherwise, you end up being *stuck* until someone maybe, if you're lucky, can come and help you out. Not a great way to go about doing things and living your life.

When I was younger, I would ride my bike all over the place, and I tell you that tubes for the wheels were *expensive!* So, if I popped a tire or something, I had to learn how to fix it *myself*. There wasn't money to go out and get a new tube. I had my own bike repair kit, and after my dad taught me how, had to put a patch on my tire myself.

Yes, *everything* that you do in life develops you as an individual. And your character and your heart, and your brain and all those things are working together to create *you* as an individual.

Like I said a second ago, it doesn't mean that you're gonna be a superstar. Not *everybody's* gonna score touchdowns. There's gotta be people around who know how to block and tackle, or else the running back ain't goin' anywhere. Or the quarterback can't throw passes, if he's getting sacked.

We all have our individual traits, our individual skills and experiences that make us who we are as people.

Still, even if you're a "worker bee," you gotta have something special going on about you, or else you'll just be a mindless person who gets up every day, goes to do the job, comes home, turns on the TV, and that's your life.

There *are* people like that, unfortunately. But I *do* think also that the fact that we've become more of a high-tech society means it's easier to be a drone 'cause you can get on your phone and scroll all day long if you want to (or all *night* long).

Then you also got a television set that's got more channels and streaming options than anybody ever had before. To a lot of people, sadly, books are kind of a thing of the past. (Hopefully not *this* one, though!)

You want *my* advice (and since you *are* reading *my* book here, I assume you *do!*), I think books are so important for kids in helping them further develop themselves into individuals who know more about life than what they see onscreen that you should take away their phones and put 'em in a room full of books!

Although we may have all this technology now that "helps" us understand the world and even ourselves "better," according to some, I still say there's something about holding a book in your hand and turning pages. That is *magic* to me 'cause what's on the next page is kinda like *what's next in your life*. Turning the next page is like wondering what you're going to do tomorrow.

Before I go off on too much of a tangent here about the importance of books, I wanna get back to the idea of creating yourself as an individual, which I also must say has to do with playing by the rules and doing the right thing. From childhood on, as you get older, you're building up your body of knowledge to make decisions. You can't do that by staring at a screen all day.

You have to buckle down and learn the right things in the right way. *Especially* while you're young, when your brain is developing and you're absorbing all this information coming at you all the time (which is why I feel so strongly about the importance of books).

You want to be an individual, but you also can't grow up saying, "Well, I'm just gonna do whatever I wanna do." I mean, you *can,* but you won't get very far, in my opinion. You have to have some basic fundamentals in your life. Everything is an accumulation of what you've learned throughout your life.

That can be book learning, it can be seat-of-your-pants learning, it can be mentors (or siblings, or older kids or your parents).

But you gotta have a good body of knowledge in order to develop your individuality, because what you take in creates the individual *you*.

COWBOY WISDOM

Son, I have *hangovers* older than you are!

REBELLION

When I hear the word "rebellion," my *first* thought that comes to my mind is the American Revolution, which was a rebellion against the status quo. The colonists figured they'd been pushed around enough, and they felt they had a right to redress their grievances.

When I think of the word "rebellion" secondarily, I think about *generational* rebellion. I'll go to the one I'm most familiar with: *Baby Boomers rebelling against their parents*. We rebelled against the Greatest Generation, and our rebellion took on the forms of smoking weed, sexual revolution and all that kind of stuff.

We were gonna spit the bit and do what we wanted to do, and "they" couldn't tell us what to do anymore. *We were gonna show 'em!*

In some respects, our parents said, "Well, you go right on ahead, and then when *you* have kids, you lemme know how that works out!"

Rebellion is a necessary part of the world, because things get to a certain point. Eventually, as with what happened with my generation rebelling against their elders, you'll *always* have a group of people in a place in which they figure they've been pushed around enough that they're gonna rebel.

I think that's not necessarily a bad thing. Unless it's just rebelling for rebelling's sake and not toward a purpose or a goal. Like when it came to the American Revolution, as mentioned, and the colonies needed to rebel against the British in order to retain and expand their human dignity and rights.

If focused properly, rebellion can work to free *everybody* from bondage.

Without a purpose, though, well . . . rebellion can become just so much noise. It becomes a case of, "All right, we're rebelling. *Now* what? What's the *plan*?" You also need to be careful and must remember that there are *consequences* to everything we do in life. Consequences for our behavior and consequences for our actions.

Unfortunately, for these newer generations, *their* parents have gotten to the point where they try to *reason* with their kids when the kids are rebelling. They do this because *older* generations of parents *didn't* reason with kids. *Our* parents threw down the law, and *the law was the law*. There were *consequences* for our rebellions. Nowadays, rebellion amongst kids is more commonplace in the sense of "the inmates running the asylum."

By that I mean that we've kinda lost control of these younger generations that like to think that they're gonna rebel and do whatever the hell they wanna do without any consequences.

It's a *choice*, really. America's made a *choice* about this. We've allowed people to "speak their truth" instead of recognizing that there is only *one* truth.

Along with *that* falsity, there's also this notion that, "My rebellion is gonna be the norm from now on." No, that's not how it works, kiddo. It's thinking like *that* that gets us away from the tight infrastructure of society. If *everybody's* out there rebelling, who's running things?

You have to have *some* continuity from generation to generation, and from government to government and from people to people.

What I'm trying to say is that it's okay to rebel and to go test yourself as an individual, but you also all gotta be pulling on the same end of the rope at some point, or all we got is anarchy.

If you have yourself a crew of cowboys out there on the range, and they're all working to gather up a whole bunch of cows, then if everybody decides to go and do it their own way, you're *not* gonna be gathering those cows up. If you're gonna rebel against the boss who told you to go to the left "out thatta way," and you say, "No, I'm going to the right *thatta* way," well, that's why he's the boss: 'cause *he* knows where the cows are, and *he* knows what you're supposed to be doing. That's when rebellion for rebellion's sake could equal *chaos*.

That's not like a group of people deciding, like in our American Revolution, that, "We are tired of being pushed around, we're tired of being overtaxed, and we have rights!"

When it comes to *personal* rebellions, well . . . how should I say this? So, I had three brothers, and they all went to the University of California, Berkeley. They all pledged the same fraternity. They all followed a pattern. Me, though? I rebelled against that. I was the fourth boy in line, and I had always had to follow my older brothers. But now that I was graduating high school, I didn't want to follow anyone anymore.

It did take me a while to find my path. There *were* consequences for my rebellion. I ran off to Europe and became a hippie for a year or so; no college, no fraternity, no *anything* aside from being out there and free and running around like a wanderer in a whole other country. It was fun, but there *were* consequences. I mean, even though I had some great adventures, I *did* lose a little time in moving forward in my life. There's gotta be a balance there, you know?

I didn't think about it as *rebelling*, at the time. I didn't think about it 'til later in life. At the time, it was a matter of my not wanting to follow all of my brothers through every stage of life. I wanted to do *something else.* I wanted to try a different path and see where it would take me.

My dad and I (surprise, surprise!): We kind of disagreed at times on that. He'd worriedly ask my mom, "When is Patrick gonna settle down? When is he gonna do this and that?" And she would say, "Let him go. He'll find what he's trying to find out there." And I did; just took me longer, and I didn't do it in a traditional way.

When I look back on it, I also always say I'm glad I did what I did, because it led me into a whole series of adventures I probably would've never had if I had stayed the path and pattern of those who had come before me.

COWBOY WISDOM

An older man said, "Erasers are made for those who made mistakes." A youth replied, "Erasers are made for those who are willing to correct their mistakes."

Believing in something makes it possible, not easy. But never stop believing.

Hope is the seed stock of happiness. Plant the seeds of hope, and reap a bountiful harvest of happiness.

IDEALISM

My dad was very optimistic, and he always used to say, "You gotta look at the bright side—even when things are darkest." And I never forgot that.

It sounds simple, but it's *tough* when things go against you, you're looking around for somebody else to blame, you're looking for what went wrong and who's at fault. Sometimes, you gotta look in the mirror. In fact, one of my mom's favorite sayings was, "If you're looking for a helping hand, start by looking at the end of your own damn arm."

Sometimes, when we're looking around at things that have got us down, we've gotta look in the mirror, we've gotta look at the end of our own hand and we gotta start helping *ourselves*.

The other thing to remember here is: *hope.* If you get up in the morning, and you don't have hope that things are gonna get better, turn in your birth certificate, because that's one horrible life to live through, if you ask me. Even if it's a bare *sliver* of hope, you gotta hold onto *something*, and *you've gotta pick yourself up*. That's the trick, really: You've gotta have *hope* that things will get better, but you can't just sit around and wait for your hopes to be realized.

It's an active thing.

It's like when people pray, "Gee, God, help me make more money next year." Well, that's not what you should be praying for. You *should* be praying for, "Give me work for my hands," *and the rewards will come.*

It's all tied together: hope, optimism. . . .

Now, *optimism* is what you get up in the morning for—you're *optimistic* that things are going to get better and that you *are* gonna do better. Relationships giving you some problems? Or do you want to get a better job situation? If you *don't* have hope and optimism, like I said a few lines back, *what exactly are you DOING here?*

Famed football coach Vince Lombardi was once quoted as having said (I'm paraphrasing), "Winning is everything." Well, that wasn't *exactly* what he meant. What he *meant* was that you have to *strive* for the best, and that though you may never reach perfection (who could?), you might just reach *excellence*. But you've gotta *work* for it. Ain't *nobody* gonna do it *for* you.

This is what it means to work toward having a successful life. You wanna be able to look back on your life when you're facing the end and say that you've lived a good and honorable life. This will allow you to look back on your life and enjoy everything you've done a *second* time before you're gone.

I've looked at *my* life and said, "Gee, the ups and downs!" Over the last year, I've experienced some pretty difficult times. I had to look at myself in the mirror and say, "What's going on? What can I do to pick myself back up again and become the person I used to be?

I mean, I won't go into details, but I knew that I had to do something.

So, I made one of the most difficult decisions I've ever made. I decided I couldn't do it myself and that I needed to find professional help. It was hard to admit. But to continue to avoid all the things in my life that I had denied and swept under the rug hoping that out of sight would be out of mind was not an option. And that's allowed me to slowly find and reacquaint myself with the person I once was.

Because what I have found out is that as long as you got something to hang on to, you can pull yourself out of *anything*. If you *don't*, it's gonna be a damn miserable existence for you.

Honestly, when you fail at marriages and relationships like I have, it ain't a good sign. But you've gotta deal with it.

Then I look at all the jobs I've had, all the bouncing around I've done. I know I've done a lot of good things, and I'm proud of that, for sure. But, there have also been times when I've felt *professionally* like a failure, too. There was one point where I even said to my brother Steve, "You know, I'm a failure. Look at me: I don't have a lot of money, I don't have a lot of *anything*. What have I done with my life?" Then Steve looked right at me and said what I needed to hear. He said, "You've done so much with your life, Patrick. Look at all the things you *have* done. Look at all the people you've met. Look at all the *lives* you've touched." He was right. It's nothing to sneeze at.

Every time *you* get down like that, you gotta get right back up again. You gotta *figure out* how to get back up again.

I've had a lot of friends lately who have been passing away. I'm getting to that age, you know? Sadly, some of these friends fell down and never got back up again.

Maybe they didn't know how.

Me, I was lucky enough to have parents who kicked my butt into gear when I needed it and would tell me, "Patrick, you gotta pick yourself up. Yeah, you can ask for help if you really need it. But that doesn't necessarily mean someone's gonna come by and help you." I've always remembered that. It's like the guy who's drowning 30 feet from shore. Sure, someone's gotta get over to him and throw him a rope, but the guy better be kicking hard and better be reaching out *for* that rope, or he'll drown. And that, to me, is idealism. That's optimism, you know? You're in trouble, you may need help, but you still reach out and kick. You still are working to keep yourself going, even during the toughest of times.

Kinda reminds me of that old Shel Silverstein cartoon where the two guys are totally emaciated and chained to the bottom of a deep, cavernous prison cell with no visible hope whatsoever of getting out, and yet one of the guys is facing the other, with the caption reading, "So, here's my plan." Tragic? Yes. Funny? Perhaps. But also very true. Even in situations like that, you gotta keep figuring out how to dig yourself out of your hole. *That's* idealism.

However you get it, you gotta reach down inside yourself and pull out whatever you got inside into your reserve tank. Even when it feels like you ain't got nothin' left!

COWBOY WISDOM

A slow dance with the right partner is one of life's sweetest pleasures.

Love is a medicine—for the one who gives it and the one who receives it. That's a good prescription for life, so give it out in healthy doses every day.

LOVE

I've not been too good with the *romantic* love part of life.

I've loved women. I've loved men—of course not in the *romantic* way, but in the way of loving them as *people*. More like how Jesus spoke about love of your fellow man. Love through *friendship*.

The guys I grew up with, we've shared a deep friendship. I like to think that although I've not been good at staying in touch over the years, it's still there. One of these guys I still talk to all the time has been a great advisor to me. He's helped me throughout my *romantic* love issues. (*I value his expertise.*) And as we've gotten older, we tend to end our conversations with, "Love you, brother."

And, I tell you what: It feels *good*.

But, like I said, as far as *romantic* love: gosh, I've not been very successful. My own *mother* said to me one time, "You're not very good at this, son, so be careful."

Sometimes I give my love too quick. I get impulsive and think, *Gee, I* love *her. Right? Uh oh, what did you just say? And do you really mean that right now? Or are you saying it, 'cause you think it's the thing to say?* And on and on like that.

This kind of thinking has gotten me into a lot of trouble. I move too quickly, haven't been as discerning sometimes as I should have been and should have waited to let things play out a little more. Which is probably why I'm single again! Like my mom said, I'm not too good at it.

With my horse Beamer, it's a whole other kind of love we're talking about. But definitely love nonetheless.

When I got Beamer, we were more or less new to each other, and I was still learning. Still am. In a way, *he* was still learning too. Because he was still healing and finishing his rehab from his injury, there were some things he couldn't do. And at the same time, *I* was broken up from my second marriage ending, from my divorce from a woman who had been fighting her demons for many years. She was an alcoholic.

My life had been a mess for *years*. When I met Beamer, though, *his* life *wasn't* a mess. He'd been kind of hanging around and was well taken care of by the women who sold him to me, Cathi and her daughter Alyssa. *But* he was looking for something, too. I think he wanted to know, "What's my purpose? What's my job?" Horses like jobs. They're workers.

Well, it turns out his job was teaching me, and not only about riding. His job was to teach me about life, and patience and taking a step into the unknown, because I was no longer dealing with my first horse, Andy, who was an eighteen-year-old horse that I could throw a saddle on and jump on with no problem. Now, with Beamer, I was dealing with a horse that hadn't been ridden regularly for a while because he was rehabbing from an injury. Well trained in cutting, his discipline, he was in need of other things to make him a better all around ranch horse.

Soon after I moved Beamer up to Idaho, I met Trudy, who was the manager of the boarding facility where Beamer was going to live. Trudy came up to me one day after she watched me ride. She said, "You ride pretty good, but you're gonna get hurt. Let me help you."

Trudy took me under her wing and really helped me. More than anything, she taught me how Beamer and I could become deeply connected to each other.

We worked hard to train him. And, because of that time and work and *love* we put into it all, a lot of things he couldn't really do before are now things that are easy for him. He knows exactly what to do.

That's largely because I learned from Trudy, through love, how to connect to Beamer. Our connection—that love—grows every time I see him, every time we're together. I really know him now, and he knows me. Now I know what he might do. I know what to do if he gets a little spooked, or whatever else may happen.

If I'm up in my saddle and not "sitting deep," so to speak, as we say, Beamer can *feel* that. He can feel a *fly* on his back. So, if he feels I'm not comfortable, he goes, "*Patrick's* not comfortable with the saddle, so *I'm* not comfortable."

While, if I sit deep and am getting myself all settled in, Beamer will go, "Ah, *there's* my guy, *there's* my leader." It's the most beautiful thing in the world.

I love him so much. Beamer has gotten me through some tough times. And I know I can always go to him and look at him and give him a treat, or just stroke him and hold him around the neck. I've *cried* doing it, because of what he's given me. He's given me some purpose. And I've given *him* some purpose. When I get out of his way, so to speak, as Trudy always tells me to do, he simply *does his thing*. Which is *also* a *beautiful* thing. When he does his thing, it's like a ride at Disneyland. *Just ride it out.*

It's *love* in that connection we have when I drive up. He puts his head over the fence and he knows it's me. He can hear my truck coming from a couple hundred yards away. When I used to live in Idaho, I had to walk a fair distance from my truck to where he was in his loafing shed and turnout. But he could hear me coming, and by the time I would get to his shed, he'd be waiting at the door.

He'd be ready for me: "What are we gonna do today, Patrick?"

"Today, Beamer, you get to run. You can go be a horse. I'm gonna let you out and run in the field."

"Okay, I'll go run in the field!"

Or it might be: "Today, Beamer, we're gonna do the saddle, because we're gonna work cows with a couple of friends."

"Great, Patrick! Terrific!"

What Beamer and I have is love, but it's also a very special connection. Our relationship gives me such great pleasure. When I moved down here to St. George, Utah, and he was still up in Idaho, I was a *mess* because I couldn't talk to him. I couldn't see him. I couldn't sit on him.

I'll let you in on a little something here: When I was breaking up with my girlfriend last year, I'd go see Beamer just to talk with him. We're not even talking about putting a saddle on him. Just me talking. One of these times, I slid open the door to his shed, and he was at the other end eating. I stood there; I didn't go towards him, I just stood there.

Beamer swings his head around to me. Now, granted, he knows I've always got treats in my pocket. But *this* time, I didn't have anything on me, because I'd forgotten. Regardless, Beamer turns from where he was eating and starts slowly walking towards me. He stops right in front of me, right in front of my face, face to face.

And I threw my arms around his neck and started to cry.

Beamer didn't move. He didn't do *anything* but let me cry with him. Let me put my smell in. I know his smell. All horses have the same smell, somebody might say; but that's *his* smell. The inside of my truck smells like that. I actually coined a phrase about this. "If the inside of your truck smells like a horse, you got a great life. If it smells like *your* horse, It's even better."

It was this feeling that he *knew* to walk up to me. He *knew* I needed him.

Maybe I'm reading into it too much, but there really did seem to be something special that day. Beamer seemed to *know* I was going through some stuff, and he left his food behind to come over and nuzzle with me.

Here was this majestic animal saying to me in his own loving way, "It's okay. I'm here for you. I've got you." That's love.

A FANCY EDUCATION MIGHT GAIN YOU SOME KNOWLEDGE, BUT ONLY HARD LIFE EXPERIENCES WILL GAIN YOU WISDOM. A PHD WON'T HELP YOU FIX A FLAT TIRE.

CSI

WEDNESDAY

THE COMMON SENSE COWBOY'S GUIDE TO LIFE

WANDERLUST

VANITY

COMPETITION

TECHNOLOGY

ART

RESPECT

COWBOY WISDOM

The farther you run away, the farther it is back. And no matter how far you run, you'll never outrun whatever you're running from.

Every sunrise is a new trail to ride. Make it count.

WANDERLUST

I got some Chinese food recently, and my fortune cookie read, "Embrace your wanderlust spirit, and come to life." I really liked that. Who knew you could get a message tailor made for you from a fortune cookie!

Wanderlust, though: I've always had it. Maybe it's why I've moved around so much and had so many different experiences in my life. Huh? For me, I don't know if it's a search for eternal youth, like if I start over, the "age" clock restarts to the beginning, or searching for something else altogether. Honestly, sometimes I don't even know what I'm looking for. For example, in romantic relationships. I've not been too successful, because I think I might have an idealized version of what I want—while life is *not* about a series of idealized versions of what you want, *especially* not in your romantic life.

I guess my problem here *is* my wanderlust, because I'll be in a relationship, and I'll think, *God, is this what I want?!* That's when I start thinking about what may lay over the next hill. I start thinking about starting the search again for where I belong and what will *really* make me happy.

So, yes, that wanderlust keeps coming up for me. Then when I *don't* have it in my life, I can't help feeling a bit like I've stopped living. The last time this happened was when I got seriously into horses and learned the cowboy way and the cowboy world. Yeah: It was *wanderlust* that helped push me into that. But while I still have that wanderlust feeling, it has changed. I no longer feel like I'm searching for where I fit. I finally know where I fit personally, it's where I belong geographically that I'm working on. It turns out where I belong is the cowboy world and the cowboy life I'm in now—a life that my mom had told me about when I was a small boy.

I think she's been guiding me to this life from above from the time she passed away, which was the catalyst for my journey. Now she's trying to help me figure out what state that is!

Then, of course, the *cowboy* has a kind of wanderlust, right? Especially in the old days, moving from outfit to outfit, taking with him only the things he could carry on his horse. What is known in the cowboy world, his "possibles." The bare necessities to survive.

A lotta that is about *always looking westward*, looking westward . . . *toward the sunset*. And I think that's what

I look for when I'm riding: *towards the sunset*. I've always said that when it's my time—when it's "the end" for me—if I knew when my expiration date was, had a terminal disease or maybe was just wearing out—I'd like to think me and Beamer could go together. I'd ride him out on the range somewhere; I'd put down a bed roll and kinda lie there and let him go off on his own before I finally end up dying. That would be the end of my wanderlust. At least I'd do it on the trail somewhere. Maybe that's a bit of a romanticized version, but . . . it's what I want.

I suppose it's the idea of not wanting to be trapped.

You know, when I've been to my high school reunions and those sorts of get-togethers, a lot of the guys I used to know worked their whole lives, and they did very well for themselves.

They had families, they had kids, they had grandkids. That was always a trap to me, because I always saw that as the beginning of the end. I know that sounds crazy, but that's what it always felt like to me. And, honestly, I felt that kind of lifestyle would *terminate* my wanderlust. To me, it feels like a kind of claustrophobia. Like, "I gotta get outta here!"

It's why I was so taken aback by that fortune cookie: Yeah, *embrace* my wanderlust and "come to [my] life." It *is* the spirit inside of me. Along with the spirit in America as a whole: Always looking for the next frontier, always looking to *explore*.

To me, we can all do it on our own level.

Now, I'm no genius, and I'm certainly not perfect; I've made enough mistakes to fill the Grand Canyon. But, as the guy at the end of the bar, I wanna let people know—especially young people—that while they're searching for where they belong, where they fit, let a little wanderlust into their life.

I wouldn't advise doing it like me necessarily!

I sometimes *envy* those guys I know who have worked and more or less stayed in the same place, raised their families and all the rest of it.

I get their Christmas cards, and I see my buddies with their families. Yeah, it can make me envious, if I'm going to be honest.

One of my best friends, someone I've known since third grade, sent me a picture of his entire extended family at Christmas—there he is, at the center of all these lives. He and I talk all the time, and I know that he feels really good about what he's done with his life. He is justly proud as he should be.

It's times like that when I wonder what would've happened if I'd done the same thing, taken the same path as these other guys.

Maybe I should have. Hmmm. . . .

Anyway . . . all of this last part is to say that I certainly don't wanna denigrate anybody who has lived that kind of life, staying in the same place, raising a family, contributing to their communities, being good citizens. After all, all of that is a lot of what keeps the world going round, and it forms the foundation of our society. Even though it can make me a little jealous—sure—it's not what I chose for my life, I am where I am now, and that works for me. I accept my choices, and I accept the *consequences* of my choices. I could've made different choices—but I didn't.

These other guys, they have the satisfaction of just being happy at how they have lived their lives and what they have accomplished. And I will happily live with the choices I have made.

But my wanderlust is never far from my mind.

COWBOY WISDOM

You can't tell how far a frog can jump by his croak. It's the same with someone who brags about how well they can do something. Until they do it, it's just words.

The sun don't rise to hear the rooster crow. Even if the rooster thinks so.

VANITY

I'm always reminded of what baseball great Reggie Jackson once said when somebody accused him of bragging and being vain. I think it was right after he hit three home runs in a World Series game. He said, "*It ain't bragging, if you can back it up.*"

To me, we *all* have a certain amount of vanity. Yeah, it's one of the seven deadly sins, but we *all* have some; we can't avoid it. We're human beings. Whether it's how we look, how we dress, our hairstyle, how we act, the words we use, how we wanna be viewed by others. We've all got some vanity about us. The *trick*, I think, is that you gotta have *pride* in what you do, but not be *prideful*.

You wanna look your best without staring in the mirror too much. (Or, at least, you don't wanna be one of those people who, every time you walk by one, you gotta look at yourself.) You gotta check yourself. Sure, you should put an aura out there where people say, "Man, *that* person's got *confidence*." But there's a fine line between being confident and doing something while being vain about it.

As the Bible says in Proverbs 16:18, "Pride goeth before destruction, and a haughty spirit before a fall." If you *do* get too vain. *You're gonna fall at some time*. And, if you're too vain and everybody notices it, are they gonna be as quick to help pick you up? Or are they gonna say, "Good! He deserved it! He was too prideful and now he's being taught a lesson?"

So again, it's a fine line between confidence and just ol' vanity for vanity's sake.

I *do* love that Reggie Jackson line, because it's true. If you can do something, you may wanna brag about it; but you don't wanna *overly* brag. Too much bragging is arrogant and downright annoying after a while.

There's an old cowboy saying that a cowboy who does too much bragging around the campfire pretty soon finds himself sitting around the campfire by himself, 'cause nobody wants to listen to all that crap. They wanna listen that you did well that day, but you should be proud *and* humble. There's that fine line I've been talking about once again. For many things in life, don't take yourself too seriously, 'cause nobody else is gonna.

Now, I keep going back to Reggie Jackson, and we all know that when it comes to sports, there's a *lot* of vanity there and a lot of extra confidence there. On one level, it's needed for them to do what they gotta do.

But on another level, *these* days, there's a lot of discussions that are going on about how to raise good boys who are gonna be strong and confident but aren't gonna be bullies.

When it comes to this kind of thing, my advice would be that one of the worst things you can do when you're competing is be arrogant and think you are the best simply because you showed up.

I'll give you an example. Years ago, I went to watch a Golden Gloves fight in San Francisco. Now in Reno, Nevada, there was an Indian school. These kids are very poor. Yet, they always found a way to show up with a team of boxers.

I had a pretty good seat with my buddy. Into the ring comes this young Black kid. At the time, Muhammad Ali was wearing tassels on his boxing shoes. And he'd be all flashy, moving his feet around real fast. This Black kid we were watching in the ring was representing the Police Athletic League in San Francisco, and he had all the great gear you could imagine on—silk trunks and all that—and he was dancing and shooting his fists around, preening and everything else.

And then, in the other corner, was this Indian kid, and *he* had on a pair of beat-up old high-top basketball shoes and a pair of gym shorts that were faded. He wasn't wearing fancy stuff. It was something right outta *Rocky*.

The Indian boy and the Black boy walked to the middle of the ring, they tapped gloves, and then the Indian boy—*boom!*—with one punch sent the other kid to the canvas. *Fight over*.

Now, the Indian boy was there to compete and do the best he could. I didn't know anything about his motivation or his background. All's I *did* know is that he walked into that ring and *flattened* the kid who was preening. And it taught me a great lesson: *If you're gonna go in the ring like a showboat, you better be able to back it up.*

When it comes to kids *today*, there's so much pressure of competing in these "super leagues," I'll call them. These kids today go from Little League to all these traveling teams, and their parents hire private coaches and all the rest of it for them. It's amazing, the cost, the time consumed. It's also amazing what this kind of thing does to kids.

It *used* to be that you'd go down to the playground, you'd pick sides, you'd play the game, and kids would be their own "referee," so to speak. If a guy slid into home plate, the *kids* were the ones who would say if he was out or not; *not* an adult.

Yes, we had Little League with parents as coaches, but I remember a lot less pressure and more fun.

Nowadays, the kids have so much pressure on them—it's not just "fun 'n games" anymore. On one level, that's great, because they're competing at a much higher level. But I can only imagine the stress they must be putting on their lives, too. The stress to achieve and to look good in front of their parents and everyone else.

It's the same with education. Not every kid's gonna be Einstein. Likewise, not every kid's gonna know how to use his hands expertly and craft a birdhouse in woodshop class. I think that the overemphasis on *competition* creates too much vanity, and it creates too many mental problems later on in life for kids who do need to learn how to *compete* but also need to learn how to *lose*.

You have to learn how to get knocked down, get up and know that next week's another game or next week's another test. Because you're gonna be tested throughout your life, whether it's in athletics or the classroom or a job. Life is a *series* of tests. And you hope that when you get to the end of your life, you get a passing grade and that you can look back and say, "I lived a pretty good life."

To me, that's more important than anything else.

Oh, and remember the opposite of vanity is humility. We could use a lot more of that today.

COWBOY WISDOM

It takes two things to do a job: To start and to finish. And always finish what you start.

Don't get mad at somebody who knows more and is better'n you at something. It ain't their fault. Instead, try learning what they know so you can get better.

When you lose, don't lose the lesson. Life is one learning experience after another. Whether you win or lose, both experiences require the same amount of work. Sometimes you win the buckle, and sometimes you don't. It's those times you *don't* that teach you the *real* lessons.

COMPETITION

Competition starts pretty early in your life. Sometimes you're competing for your parents' attention with siblings, for one thing. Then you start going school, and there's definitely a sense of competition *there*. And not necessarily in *sports*, but other avenues as well, competing with your fellow students.

Sometimes even *your parents* are judging you by that competition. "Why aren't you doing as well as so-and-so?" they may ask (or wonder to themselves without saying it aloud). Maybe more internally within the family, like, "Why aren't you doing as well as your brother did when he took that class?"

And, boy, once I got into the cowboy lifestyle, this idea of competition became even harder for me to deal with. Mainly because I didn't grow up in the lifestyle, and so many other people I'm interacting with *did*. I've watched how these folks born into the saddle compete, and I've watched how they handle themselves in competition.

Now, sure, I've won a couple of buckles in competition, which is a measuring stick, if you will. But the one thing I notice about the *non*-cowboy world when people compete in sports or whatever it might be: there's such a cutthroat attitude! You're gonna *stomp* the person you're competing with. That's the whole point, isn't it? That's what people think and feel most of the time outside the cowboy world.

Back *in* the cowboy world, though—at rodeos, reining, cutting, roping or sorting competitions things like that—there's a lot more camaraderie in competing with each other. You can call it "sportsmanship" if you like.

There's not so much "trash talk" or making fun of your opponent. In fact, when I first started doing cow work, I was really worried people would laugh at me or judge me harshly, since I was still so new to it all. But that wasn't the case when I actually dove into it. In fact, things were totally the opposite.

They even have a wonderful term to this effect, the idea of encouraging folks who are giving their best effort. They might say something like, “That boy or girls got ‘try.’” Meaning you’re giving it all you got. And what I’ve learned is that try plus skill equals success. But skill without try won’t get you there.

Like this one time I’ll never forget when it was my first cow sorting competition. My partner and I did okay but not enough to win. I knew I hadn’t done very well. This older cowboy who ran the competitions at his arena pulls me aside and he goes, “Let me give you a few tips.” It wasn’t, “God, you’re shitty, Patrick! What are you even *doing* here?” No. It was about him wanting to help me to get better. Then I *did* get better. And, on top of that, I started going to more competitions at his place—every *week*, in fact!

On top of *that*, after a while, the same guy says to me, “You got it. You just need to keep practicing.” It was the idea that, at least in the cowboy world, *nobody’s giggling if you’re screwing up.* Because they know you’re giving it your “try,” you’re giving it your best. It’s a much better situation than what we see so often in the non-cowboy world where—yeah—people don’t just want to *beat* you; they want to *beat you into the GROUND!*

My trainer Trudy once told me that if I mess anything up, just tell people, “I’m working on it.” Because, in the end, in the cowboy world, everybody—even those in competition with each other—is looking to *help* each other out, you know? You don’t look down on people who are competing with you. You make sure that everybody’s part of the whole competition and feeling good about what they’re doing.

There was another time when I won a buckle at a small event. There was an old cowboy, my friend Jim Parker, who was there when me and my two partners won the buckles for the cow competition. Jim and his late wife Patty were champion team ropers together, and Jim had cowboyed all over the West. About a week later, I saw Jim and Patty at a team roping competition, and he asked me, "Patrick, how you doing?" I told him I was doing pretty good. We had a little more small talk, but then he looked down at my belt, and he asked me where my new buckle I'd won was.

I told him, "Ah, gee, Jim. I don't know. I'm kind of embarrassed about it, actually. I'm not like all these great cowboys who have won events so much bigger than mine, and here I am walking around all these guys who are so darn good at all this stuff."

Jim then says to me a little sternly, "Son, you *won* that buckle. Wear it and be proud of it. You competed, and you won."

I'll never forget that. It doesn't matter if you won it for winning the National Finals Rodeo (NFR) in Las Vegas, or you won it for a small competition with a bunch of other ranching cowboys. You worked at it, and you competed, and you gave it "try." And that, to me, is the essence of the whole damn thing.

When it comes to teaching *kids* about competition, I think it's important to make it clear to them that there's *winning* and there's *losing*. Not everyone gets a prize—or at least *shouldn't* get a prize! You compete, you work hard, and you *win*. Or, you do your best and you *lose*. That happens, too. We need to instill this system of reality in our children, or else the whole idea of competition will completely collapse. *Then* where will we be?

I remember when I was playing Little League, and I came home after a game, with my dad asking me how it had gone. “We lost,” I told him.

He said to me, “Huh. How’s it feel?”

I told him it didn’t feel too good.

“Okay, “he continued. “What does *that* mean?”

I’m just a kid, shuffling my feet and telling him, “I’m mad that we lost.” (*My Dad always asked you questions when teaching you a life lesson.*)

Well, of *course* I was mad! But, also, losing is just another part of life. My Dad explained it pretty well as I remember. He said, “Well, first you’re gonna have to work harder if you want to win next time. And second, you have to *accept* the fact that you’re not gonna win every time. You’re *not*. But *that doesn’t mean that you don’t try*.”

Kids should be allowed to be kids. Absolutely. But, again, I think you have to have some kind of measuring stick of success and failure, if you teach children at a young age how to deal with both, they will be much better off. They’ll learn, young, how to handle both winning *and* losing. They’ll learn early on, as I like to say, that you can either “cowboy up” or you can “go sit and cry in the truck.”

Look, sometimes you don’t win. Sometimes you don’t “make it.” *That ain’t the end of the world*. Maybe. Maybe the thing you’re trying to do isn’t necessarily for you. Maybe there’s something *else* that’s your calling in life. Maybe it’s something *else* that you’re supposed to be doing, something *else* you'd be more successful at. And *that's* an important lesson to learn, too.

COWBOY WISDOM

Old roads, old dogs, old folks and old ways still have a lot to offer in this sped-up world we live in.

If it ain't broke, chances are it *will* be. Everything breaks sooner or later. So, learn how to fix it.

TECHNOLOGY

Just as is the case in a *lot* of different vocations or lifestyles, there's the older cowboys who are not particularly *against* technology but do feel there's simply "certain ways you do things." For example, you're not gonna figure out a new way to brand a calf. You gotta go rope it, drag it to the fire and brand it. *Period.*

Yeah, you might use an ATV to go drive out and fix a line of fences and check if there's any holes. But you know something? It's a heck of a lot more fun to go fix fences while riding a *horse*. So, right now on some of the big ranches, you might see cowboys using ATVs to gather cows, 'cause they have *thousands* of them and it's easier that way. *But* the old way of doing it on horseback is still ever-present on plenty of *other* ranches across America.

As far as "everyday technology," *everybody's* got a cell phone these days, *including* cowboys. You *need* one out there.

Let's say you're having to do some work, counting cows or something; you just doctored a cow, maybe. You look at the ear tag for the cow number, because you wanna make a record of what you did. Well, you got a phone, so you can use *that* instead of pulling out a pad of paper and pencil from your dirty and well-worn shirt pocket.

There's that old scene of a cowboy with a pencil. He licks the lead on the pencil when he writes something down in his book. Well, you know, now he might pull out his phone and do the same thing.

Then you go to a rodeo, and everybody's taking pictures. Let's say you wanna film your buddy who's doing a run, with a team roping. So, you film it for 'em, and then afterwards you go, "Well, look what happened here. The cow turned *left*." (Or whatever it may have been.) So, again, cowboys like to use cell phones, too—they do enhance things.

When it comes to doing work out in the field, if you're out there riding and something happens to you, you've got an emergency beacon on your phone, and somebody's gonna be able to find you.

So, yes, I think new technology like this *can* be an aid but, again, there's certain things that you're *not* gonna change. You can't change the way you do *some* of the work.

Buddy, *shoveling manure still takes a manure fork*. You know what I mean?

Saddling your horse still takes *saddling your horse*. And riding out to gather cows? You *can* do it a new way. But, there ain't *nothing* like the old way.

There's certain things that *are* The Way.

Cowboy's gonna adapt, though. That's why they will endure: because they will adapt and use the technology they need. *While* understanding that there's just certain things you *gotta* do the old way.

Personally, I would like to follow my dad's example: Embrace young people, learn from them.

Whenever he went to an intergenerational party, my dad would attract young people.

What my dad would be talking with young folks about was never that "when-I-was-your-age" garbage. He was interested in what *they* were doing, and he'd ask them and inquire about their lives. And he wasn't afraid of new technologies at all. Being a doctor, he knew how technology had changed his profession over the years and was fascinated by it.

I'm doing that kind of thing right now.

I'll watch these kids and be listening to them and *learning* from them. Especially when I watch them use technology to conduct maybe their own personal business or at a job where they have to know how to use technology.

I went to the feed store yesterday to buy some grain for Beamer. There was a young woman behind the counter, and we were joking around, and I tapped my card through the thing that beeps from the little chip.

The young woman, she says, "Isn't it *amazing* where we are today? I saw this movie with my mom the other day, and you guys used to have to use a piece of paper and roll with this stupid-looking thing to process a credit card."

And I said, "Yeah, we sure did! And guess what else?"

She goes, "What?"

I said, "We had these phones where we had to turn a big wheel around to call anyone."

And, of course, the young woman behind the counter laughed.

Now, we're never gonna live *completely* in their world. But I would still say we should embrace the youth and be open to new technologies.

If you get a pacemaker, you're really gonna embrace it!

The second thing I can tell you about all of this is: *It's going to happen*—the world's gonna change. It always has.

We're soon getting to the point where we'll be able to put a chip in our head that'll drive the car *for* us! I mean, heck: We already have self-driving cars. We've got all *kinds* of different things that, ten years ago, those were just a *dream*.

I remember when I was in the power business as the head of communications for the California Independent System Operator, back during the California Energy Crisis of 2000. There were reporters asking why we were using so much more electricity now than, say, 20 years ago. Well, I'd tell them that was 'cause *everything* runs on electricity nowadays! All your computers, TVs and phones and everything else.

Back then, I'd be talking about how someday we'd be able to use our phones to program our air conditioning ten minutes before getting home so that the house would be cool without our having to keep the air conditioning on all day. The reporters would say, "Aww, that's *crazy*!" But it happened, right?

Which is why the final thing I'll say on the topic of technology is: *You just have to accept it; embrace it, live the best life you can using it.*

Enjoy it and say to yourself, "I wanna live long enough to see where this is gonna take us in a positive direction." That's what *I* would say.

Enjoy the journey, look to the horizon and keep your eyes focused on the future. That's what will keep you young. That's what will be more rewarding. And embrace the young people like I do, because, if you do, maybe like me, you, too, will become more and more in awe of what they're doing and where they're going.

COWBOY WISDOM

The greatest work of art you'll ever see is the sun coming up in the morning over the prairie and setting at night over the mountains, all painted by the hand of God.

ART

When I was much younger, I would spend hours by myself drawing and perfecting voices. For example, we had a record of Bugs Bunny in the "Tortoise and the Hare" story. And I used to imitate the voices.

But what I *really* liked to do at that time in my early life was draw a lot. In the little town where I lived back then, they had competitions to paint the windows of the local merchants for Halloween. One year, a buddy of mine and I were picked to paint the window of the dry cleaners. We painted this red devil who had the face of one of the characters the renowned cartoonist Don Martin in *MAD Magazine*, which was very popular in those days, especially with boys.

I've always liked art as far as music goes, too. I played the piano when I was young. I took piano lessons; it was drilled into me pretty hard. When I got to my pre-teens (early teens, actually), I was in a little band, and I did that probably through my sophomore year in high school. I played the keyboards, and we had a bass player, a drummer and a guy who played guitar really well. He later became a professional musician and was very successful.

So, I've *always* appreciated art.

When I lived in Washington DC, especially when I was by myself after my wife moved away, I'd go to art galleries a lot. There was one gallery I'd go to over and over again, the National Portrait Gallery. It's always so quiet there, and I could just walk around for hours and hours. I'd look at my watch and say, "God, I've been here for two-and-a-half hours!" I love the realist paintings they have there. American history.

Now that I'm out West again, I'm rediscovering that whole scene. Frederic Remington and Charles M. Russell. Big, sweeping vistas of the West. And pen and ink drawings of grizzled old cowboys. I really like that kind of stuff. I have a lot of books on all that, because I'm also a book collector.

I'm a member of the Folio Society, which reprint classic books that you can buy. They're very expensive, but over the years, I've built a huge collection of 'em along with some leather-bound books from other collections, too. My collection has become very eclectic, but they're mostly classics.

Now, I've weeded some out over the years, 'cause I kept carrying 'em around from place to place that I've moved and needed to make some room. But I still keep a lot of 'em around, and in my office, I have a Churchill section, a section of great English writers, *The Decline and Fall of the*

Roman Empire, a whole area of works by Marcus Aurelius and the writings of Julius Caesar, a section on the West, history.... I like being in my office, surrounded by my books and pictures of Western art.

It's important to have a connection to art like that, because, throughout the centuries, art's been an expression of the world of that time when the art was created. Even if you go back to caveman art—whether it's guys hunting, or crude stick people or whatever it is—it's an expression of where were at that time as a growing society.

As we kept moving forward, that expression of society moved forward, too. Look at art from Ancient Rome. Or the artwork in tombs for old pharaohs telling stories from *that* time, too.

It's the same if you fast-forward to movies (or I guess I should say *films*, right?). You can watch them and see how they reflect the times in which they were made.

That's really what art's all about. Even Andy Warhol painting a Campbell Soup can is art to some people. Although why anybody would pay good money for a painting of a can of soup I have no idea! That's because art always goes parallel with civilization. It reflects what civilization is at that time.

As far as getting into art *yourself*, I would say find out what you like to do the best in that field. Do you like to draw? Try it. Some things, *you just gotta try*. So, you try it and see what your talent level is. If you're a writer, you know: *write!* And don't just start off trying to write a great Stephen King novel or something like that, because that's not who *you* are or what *you* do. Try and be somebody different. If you're trying to write columns, don't try to be George Will. If you're in radio, you're not a Rush Limbaugh, so go and try to figure out who *you* are in radio and go be *that*. That's what I did with my radio show.

Whatever the art is you want to do, if you think you got some talent, *give it a try*.

Some people think, *Oh, artists just kind of* do it. No, they have to have *discipline* to do it. They have to decide they're gonna put time into it and be ready to listen to criticism. It's the same with doing radio. It's the same with writing. It's the same with photography. You gotta put the *effort* into it. Nothing's gonna come easy.

And, you know what? Even if you *do* put the effort in, you might never sell one piece. You might never have one podcast that works. But you *can* say to yourself, "I said I was gonna do it, and I did it." And *that,* to me, is a total life lesson for *anything,* including art.

COWBOY WISDOM

Respect yourself enough to walk away from anything that no longer serves you, grows you or makes you happy.

Seek respect, not attention. It lasts longer.

RESPECT

The first thing that comes to mind is respect for *yourself*. If you don't respect *yourself*, nobody *else* is gonna respect you

And the second thing is respect for *others*.

Respect who they are, respect where they've come from, respect their experiences, respect them as people.

When you're a *kid*, you gotta show deference to older people, you know? Gotta respect your elders.

I come from the generation of "Yes, ma'am," "No, ma'am," "Yes, sir," "No, sir" whenever we went to somebody's house. It wasn't "Hi, Marge!" No, it was, "Hi, Mrs. Smith," "Hi, Mr. Smith" or maybe "Hi, Dr. Smith," whatever their title might have been.

That's that early sign of respect, which you need to learn. It's like tying your shoes—something that you need to learn when you're young, so that it's second nature in your life.

Honestly, this is one thing that kind of bugs me about some—certainly not all—young people today and I gotta say that it doesn't come from *them*, 'cause no kid is *born* disrespecting their elders. It's *learned behavior*. Which is why we gotta start with respect for elders in the beginning; it's one of the *basics* if you wanna fix the youth of America, the way everybody keeps talking about doing.

Respect. Boom: There you go. From the get-go. That's how you're gonna get kids to do the right things as they grow older. If they're taught respect at a young age, as their leash gets longer and eventually gets detached and they're on their own, they're gonna look at life a little differently than if they were raised as brats with no respect. Because don't forget: Bratty kids turn into bratty *adults*.

Respect for others also means respect for others' *lifestyle*. Don't think you're better than anybody else, 'cause you're not. You might have different experiences. You might've come from totally different places. It doesn't matter. *Nobody* is better than anyone else. And if you think you are, you're heading for a fall. And if you disrespect others, everybody's gonna look at you thinking, *That guy's a son of a bitch!*

When *that* happens, you're not gonna be included in stuff. You're not gonna have any real friends, and you might not know it, but it's a sign you don't respect *yourself*.

It's important, because learning self-respect is like learning self-reliance. It's the same thing. Learn how to rely on yourself, learn how to respect yourself.

Now, if you're dealing with some personal issues, like you're overweight or drinking too much or having issues with your relationships, you gotta come to grips with the fact that there's only one person who can fix that. And that person is the one who you look at every morning in the mirror.

It's good to seek help if you're really struggling. But the first thing you can do is learn to respect yourself as you are.

I got to a point after my time in Washington, DC, when I was pretty overweight. I looked like crap. I even had a *doctor* who told me, if I didn't change my lifestyle I would shorten my life. So, I had to look in the mirror and say to myself, "I don't like this. I don't like what I see when I look at me. And the only person who can start the process of looking, feeling and being better is *me*."

Can other people help you along the way? You bet! But you gotta help *yourself* first. And you'll be amazed to see how many people are willing to help you if you *do* start helping yourself *first*.

That comes down to *loving* yourself first, *respecting* yourself first. You gotta say to yourself, "I am who I am, and I like me!"

It's about getting up on your hind legs and saying, "Damn it, I'm gonna do something about this. I'm going to work to fix myself and make myself better."

It's also about understanding that though you can work to fix yourself, there are *no quick fixes*. Sure, for something like weight loss, you could take Ozempic if you want. Go ahead and take it. But just know that there will be consequences, as will be the case with *anything*. There's no such thing as a free lunch. There are side effects to *everything* in life. There are *trade-offs*.

Have money problems? Well, you can choose to rob other people, choose to be a crook. Okay, that might work for a while. But again: *there will be consequences to that choice*. You might end up in jail or even *killed*. Everything in life brings with it *consequences*. There are no easy outs in this life. It takes *work* to fix yourself. It takes *work* to have a better life, to find love, to lose weight, to rectify your financial situation, to work on your mental health.

Back to the *kids*; I feel really bad for them these days. The suicide rate amongst the youth are up, and it's gotten harder and harder for 'em to look in the mirror, because there's so much that's so screwed up right now. I feel sorry for 'em, for everything that's been going on in the world nowadays.

As we all know, the dark side of *technology* certainly doesn't help. All the abuse that goes on in cyberspace. Used to be that some coward could bully you on the playground, and you could pop him in the nose. *These* days, the kids are getting bullied *online,* and there's not much they can do about it, which is why it can so often sadly lead to suicide on the part of the victim of the bullying.

Which is why I say again that so much of this goes back to teaching kids respect *early*. It's all tied together. *Everything* is all tied together. *Nothing* happens in a vacuum.

But, respecting *yourself* . . . I can't say it enough times: That is *key*.

There was one time with Beamer when I had hurt my elbow. As I was swinging my saddle to throw it on his back, I felt a stabbing pain in the elbow and I dropped the saddle. Beamer got scared and, shortly thereafter, he didn't want to go back to the same area where I'd been saddling him for four years straight. It made me lose my confidence in riding and in myself.

It was such a hard thing, because I had scared my horse, and when you scare your horse, it's hard to get him back to where he'd been before. Confidence is so important. You're supposed to be the one who he trusts. If you're not confident in yourself, and something out there happens, the horse will be able to tell that you're not okay, and he might run off, dumping your ass and leaving you behind.

On the other *hand*, if you're calm and confident in yourself, and something out there goes awry, the horse may still get a little spooked but not as bad as if he doesn't think you're a good leader and have it all together.

Back to my story: Because I was in such a tough state, even after I got some therapy on my elbow and some cortisone shots, I was relying on Trudy's son Paul to saddle up Beamer. Even though I *should've* been doing it *myself*. Even though my elbow was doing better, I was still scared, since I'd had lost that confidence I'd had before. And Trudy knew what was happening. She could tell I had lost my confidence not only in saddling but in other things.

One day, Trudy had had enough. We brought Beamer back to where I'd been saddling when the aforementioned incident had taken place. I asked her, "Well, okay, where's Paul to help saddle?"

Trudy goes, "We're not playing this game anymore. *You* are gonna saddle him *yourself* again. Like you *always had.*"

She says, "Paul isn't here, and you're gonna do it totally on your own again." I was scared to do it without Trudy's son Paul's help, even though my elbow was much better, but Trudy told me I needed to cowboy up and that it was time to get back into saddling Beamer completely on my own.

I threw the saddle pad on, grabbed my saddle, and—boom!—I popped it on there. Then Trudy goes, "There: Now, finish cinching him up." And when I got it all done, I was overjoyed.

Trudy looked at me and smiled, asking, "How's that feel?"

I said, "I can't *tell* you how it feels, it feels so good."

Trudy tells me that's good and then says, "Let's go ride. Let's go get the *rest* of your confidence back." And that's what we did.

It was one of the most beautiful moments of my whole life.

I had found my self-respect right where I'd left it. In myself.

THERE IS RIGHT, AND THERE IS WRONG. THERE ARE NO LOOPHOLES, AND THE ONLY THING IN BETWEEN ARE EXCUSES.

THURSDAY

THE COMMON SENSE COWBOY'S GUIDE TO LIFE

PARENTHOOD
EMPLOYMENT
HEALTH
RESILIENCE
FAITH
WEALTH

COWBOY WISDOM

Pickles and people are sweet or sour, depending on whether they were soaked in sugar or vinegar when they were small.

When you give a lesson in meanness to a critter or person, don't be surprised if they learn the lesson. It's the same with kindness.

If your kids are bugging you to buy them a horse, first take them to a stable and see how they handle a manure fork. If they aren't willing to do that chore happily, they aren't ready for the responsibility of a horse. And you can save yourself a lot of money!

PARENTHOOD

I think that parenthood is one of the most vital elements of a free society.

Because we're talking here about raising the nation's children, and by doing so, raising the future of the nation.

It's about ensuring the nation's gonna survive.

I have nothing but respect for people that do it—taking on the responsibility of bringing new life into the world, nurturing it and eventually having to *let it go* and let them live their own life.

Realistically, we're in a world now where getting a divorce is much easier than it used to be and where we have more broken families. Hell, even *I've* been divorced twice. But I didn't have any *kids*.

Now, before you say it, I gotta interject here by saying that I can still talk about this topic, because—hey—just because I've never *played* professional football doesn't mean I can't *talk* about it!

I mean I can make observations, but I am not going to tell the coach what plays to call. And I am not going to tell parents how to raise their kids.

Being a parent *is* the most noble profession in the world. With all humility, I tip my hat and bow to those who have done it, because *I* didn't do it. When I talk about this kind of thing, I'm merely offering what I hope could be some sage guidance from a lifetime of *watching* parents.

The first ones I got to watch were *my own* and I had a front row seat.

As far as *my* parents, well . . . I always had good relations with them. I was much closer to my mother. I was the last boy, and so we had a very special bond ever since I was born. That was also because I was sick when I was a baby, and my mom had to care for me extra hard. I had to stay in the hospital right after birth because of an ear infection, which in the 1950s could have caused severe problems. She drove to the hospital every day and nursed me until I was cleared to go home. I also think she saw some of her dad in me. Her dad had a good sense of humor and was a bit of a *rogue*.

I don't know how she did it, but she made each one of us feel special in our own way and treated us as individuals, each one unique. She also bonded us together to look out for each other. For her to have been able to do that was pretty remarkable.

In high school, when I would have a home track meet at our field (I ran varsity track in the hurdles) and my brother Rob, who was eighteen months older than I, would have a home baseball game across the way (Rob played varsity baseball), my mom would go watch my race and then go watch my brother bat. I don't know how she did it all.

We all had to obey the same rules. She didn't bend rules for any of us. She didn't play favorites. She loved us all in her own special way. She laid down the law, which you didn't dare break. If you did, you would suffer the consequences. She was fair but as tough as saddle leather perhaps because she had to grow up fast, and what she learned on her sister's ranch as a young girl.

Damn, I miss her.

My *dad* was a doctor, and he worked very hard to provide the best life possible. And oh, did he.

My dad was a physical medicine and rehabilitation *specialist* who treated paraplegics, quadriplegics, children with cerebral palsy and adults with strokes. He also worked with children who had polio. Polio was a major health crisis in the 1940s and '50s before there was a vaccine. He had trained in polio treatment at Warm Springs, Georgia, where President Franklin Roosevelt—who had polio—was treated.

He used to travel throughout California, making his way to different clinics, since polio was still pretty prevalent at the time.

I don't want you to think that we never saw him or that he was too distant, though. Far from it. He was just driven by his profession and fulfilling a need in society. But, he *was* traveling up and down the Central Valley of California on foggy nights a lot. If he had gotten into a car accident, we'd have been in trouble. My mom probably would have had to go back to work, and we probably would've had to sell the house. So, it was a lot of pressure for my dad. Still, he was able to keep his own special relationship with each one of us kids, too.

Even though he worked so hard with his practice in San Francisco and traveling all around to the clinics, we always knew he was *there* for each one of us even though he couldn't always be *there*. My mom would tell us, "Your dad can't make every ball game. He can't come and watch every track meet. *But* . . . he's *there* with you. And the reason he's out there working is so that you guys can go to college and not have to work to pay for it like he did." And that's just what he did.

Now, sometimes we'd have a family meeting and, not too often, vote on something. Dad would say, "Okay, we're gonna have a meeting. We'll have a vote." Then all of us kids would vote in a block. *Then*, being the "benevolent dictator," (*his term!*) my *dad* would vote, and *somehow* his vote would always cancel *ours*.

Me, I was a rebel. I had wanderlust, as I've said. I wasn't gonna follow my brothers all the way to the same college and pledge the same fraternity and everything else. It just *wasn't* gonna happen. And in a lot of cases, my mom protected me, I would say, from my dad. I don't mean that my dad was mad or anything like *that*. He would just . . . he'd get *frustrated* with me: "When's this kid gonna *do* something with his life? What's he *doing?*" And my mom would say, "Never mind. Don't worry. He's gonna be *fine*."

It wasn't until later in my life when my dad—who loved to write letters—sent me a letter and told me how proud he was of me. That was a kind of culmination of years of my wanderlust (temporarily curbed but definitely not cured!), after which I finally settled down and got some big government jobs in Washington.

My dad knew each one of us—he knew our strengths, and he knew our weaknesses. My mom did, too. My mom was much more demonstrative than my dad, but they *both* gave us a solid foundation. They loved each other deeply and were married for 66 years before my mom's death.

Was it an idyllic childhood? Pretty close.

When my parents sold the house that we'd all grew up in and that my mom had picked out to raise her family, we had a little party. We were getting our parents settled into their new condo, and my mom gave us each a key to the old house we'd grown up in. Each one had a tag attached to the key and on the tag, written in my mom's handwriting it said, "A key to a happy childhood."

I still have my key somewhere.

COWBOY WISDOM

There's no time to rest when there's work to be done. Eat on the run, forget about sleep, and change horses often.

May you always have a stall to clean, a manure fork for your hands to do it with, and a horse that will appreciate it!

Make yourself useful. If you can't weave a blanket, mend a sock. The world needs both weavers and menders. Probably more menders.

EMPLOYMENT

Especially in the *political* world, which I was in for many years, when the campaign ends, and your guy doesn't make it (or, often, even if he *does*) or he drops out, or whatever it might be, you're kind of left flat-footed, if you know what I mean. It's abrupt. In cases like that, you better have a network to fall back on to find work.

It's true also with more *conventional* jobs where you're working for some company and think you're gonna be there a while, and then—boom!—comes the big layoff. Or maybe you get crossways with the boss, and that's the end of *that*.

In *my* experience, I've never gotten crossways with the boss. But I *did* at a point get crossways with the *government*.

During the California electricity crisis of 2000, I was the lead communications person for the California Independent System Operator.

We had been running the grid under California's new deregulation law. And for the first couple years of our operating the grid, nothing went wrong. It was easy. I thought I was gonna be living a pretty cushy lifestyle—a little media work here, a little media work there. I was getting a great salary, a 401(k), the benefits and everything else.

But then that energy crisis hit, and all of a sudden we went from "peace in our time" to DEFCON 4, and the energy system was basically being held together with spit and sealing wax.

It was in bad shape. It had been like a *lot* of things in California: It hadn't been cared for in *years*. The power plants were 50 years old. There hadn't been a new transmission line built in far too long. And, meanwhile, California was still *exploding* in population. Silicon Valley comes along, which was probably the most electricity-intensive business ever to come to California.

Long story short, I did my job and did it *very* well—including doing interviews across the *world* from the BBC to Tokyo radio and TV. Which is why we had so much national media focused on what was going on in California. I can tell you we were getting attacked from every which way as the "new guys on the block." All about how, "You don't know what you're doing! Why did California ever deregulate?" You know, all that Monday-morning quarter-backing. The real blame should have been directed at the politicians who had come up with this goat rodeo!

I held three press conferences or three press briefings every day. I was talking to media from across the globe for six to eight months. I worked seven days a week.

Through all of it, I did what I was paid to do, and I defended my people. I told the *truth*. I said, "It ain't our fault. We're not the ones who built this crummy system. We're not the ones who established a market that doesn't work. That was the *government*."

Well, the governor at the time, Gray Davis (who later got recalled in part because he screwed up the energy crisis) and his people were mad at me about what I was saying. "What are you *doing*, Patrick?"

I said, "What do you *mean*, what am I doing? I'm telling the *truth*. What? Do you expect me to *lie?*"

I had this media friend media friend who was the Governor's communications director and who I also knew from the political world, and he told me that the governor had been saying I might want to think about whether or not I wanted to keep my job. In so many words. Which sounded like an open threat to me.

So, I had to move on from that job. Leave with my head held high or get fired.

Fortunately, there was an energy company from Atlanta that had bought a bunch of California power plants, and they hired me right up. Once again, they were paying me a lot of money, including at one point something like $2 million in stock options. They just kept giving me money, because they were *making* money hand over fist.

Then the bottom fell out, some legal stuff happened to 'em, and they went bankrupt. They had been promising me the sun and the moon, but I tell you what: *They didn't even deliver a shovel full of dirt.*

I went from $2 million in stock options, a nice, big six-figure salary and a 401(k) to *nothing*. Got wiped out in probably a week. Which meant I had to go figure out what I was gonna do next. I went to work for Hill & Knowlton, a PR firm, for a while. Through *that,* I was able to keep building my network and my career and keep going pretty much as long as I wanted.

Which is why, yeah, my first piece of advice to people dealing with, or concerned about, losing their jobs would be to make sure you have a network out there. Even if you are working in a garden-variety nine-to-five situation, you better make sure you meet people throughout your industry, so that you can find somewhere to land if things end up not working out. *Always* be networking. *Always* be making sure you have something to fall back on.

Sometimes you gotta be a *hustler*, especially if you're a nomadic kinda person like yours truly. You gotta find out how to do it all *yourself*. How to get that next job *yourself*.

By the end of my career, I hadn't filled out an application or passed my resume around for a long, long time, because I didn't need to. I had my network. People knew me, and they knew what I could do, and whenever a job ended, I was always able to find something else.

Incidentally, I don't mean "hustle," like you're *lying* to people and trying to sell them "some land for condos in a Florida swamp" or anything. I mean "hustle" like you gotta be out there networking all the time, *even when you* have *a job*, because nothing lasts forever. And you better be ready to put yourself out there.

When I got into the media world, I wanted to get a radio show going. I had already been doing political commentary on this radio station in Sacramento KFBK, which is where Rush Limbaugh started. And, I tell you, I kept *hustling* 'em, kept *working it*, and I kept *begging* 'em, and I finally got my own show. They gave me a weekend show, and they gave me some sponsors, too. I did have to find some of my *own* sponsors, also. So, the hustling kept on going. Yes, even *after* I had a job.

Whether you're nomadic or *not*, you gotta think like an itinerant cowboy. Always be considering another outfit to hook up with.

All you need with you are your saddle, your chaps, your hat and your bed roll. Throw it all in the wagon, go to work, and ride for the brand.

If you're a *good* cowboy, you'll *always* find work. You're not gonna get rich at it, but you'll always be able to feed yourself.

COWBOY WISDOM

Enjoy your 20s, 30s, and 40s because in your 50s that "check engine light" comes on. And I can tell you from personal experience, by the time you get to your 60s and 70s, you're either replacing major parts or those parts are no longer available.

Life is like a cow pasture: It's very hard to get through it without stepping in some muck. Just be sure to take off your boots before you walk in the house, or you'll find out how hard life can get.

HEALTH

All these health fads!

Like Mark Twain said, "Don't read too many health books: you could die of a misprint."

All jokes aside, I've not been a great practitioner of good health over the years myself. I'm doing better now, and working on it more these days, but when I left Washington, DC, and moved back to California for a spell a while back, I was in *crummy* shape.

I had gotten divorced from my first wife. And I just wasn't taking very good care of myself. I ended up going to a doctor, and he goes, "Oh, my gosh: your blood pressure's high!" (And all this *other* stuff, too.)

So, I went to a gym, walking in and saying, "I'm willing to do *anything*. I want to get *right*." The folks at the gym, they told me I needed a trainer and to get on a good nutrition program and all the rest of it. I told them, "Let's do it."

And I invested in myself. It was expensive, but I did it. In addition to my exercise routine, I took on a twelve-week food program—they gave me specialized menus, and I had to write down everything I ate every day. *Accountability*.

I went from 25% body fat to 10%.

It was a wonderful feeling of getting healthy, of "I'm doing it *right* this time."

Then, some years later, when I came down to St. George, Utah, I had my bad elbow, which led me to neglect working out as much; the only thing I was really doing was riding.

So, once again, I said, "Okay, I gotta get myself right, and I gotta get my health back." Because, no matter where you're at in your life or what you're doing (or even what impediments or inconveniences you might be dealing with), it's important that you do whatever you can to stay healthy.

I don't think you have to go to a gym, *necessarily* but it's *so* important to keep moving, keep walking, being as active you're able to be.

It's a shame the way things have changed. If you look at pictures of people on the beach in the '60s, you don't see a lot of obese people. *Nowadays*, you don't see a lot of *skinny* people.

I'm just gonna say it: This country has become disgustingly obese. It's sad that we've allowed this to happen. You go to buy something to eat at any chain restaurant, and they give you an oval plate overflowing with food—*way* too much.

Then there are those who decide to go to the *other* extreme and say, "Gimme Ozempic so I can lose the weight!" Between McDonald's and Ozempic, *somebody's* making a lot of money.

Whatever the case, when it comes to physical health, you're either taking care of yourself or you're *not*. If you're *not*, you're gonna pay the consequences. You're gonna have a shorter life. And that life of yours is not going to be as comfortable as it could be. You also might not end up getting to see your grandkids grow up (or at all).

We all make choices. Taking care of yourself *is* a choice. I do wish more people would make a better choice. Especially right now, when it seems like lots of people are drinking a heck of a lot more than they used to, too.

Another sin I am guilty of at times in my life.

It's good to know—that said—that there's also a sobriety movement amongst young people today. I read that some Gen Zers are embracing a "sober curious" or just plain sober lifestyle, either drinking less or not at all. The young woman who cuts my hair, she's 23 years old, a little independent entrepreneur—*and* she doesn't drink.

She goes, "I don't need it."

In such ways as this, I think younger people are gonna be the examples going forward 'cause they're watching what's happened in previous generations, and they're taking it all in.

Mental health is something we *all* struggle with, as well.

Now, I have never addressed some of the issues I should have addressed when I was with my first wife (and probably before that, too), if I'm gonna be honest. Then when I moved down to St. George after *another* breakup, *another* personal failure at a relationship. I asked myself, *Why does this keep happening? I've gotta do something about this.* Made me think of how my ex, Michele, had told me, it might be a good idea to get some *therapy. Turned out she was right.*

That can be hard to do. Particularly for a lot of *men*, who are thinking to themselves, *I don't need to do that.* Is that really true, though?

In fact, I'm finding more and more people I know (including men who I respect) to have done it, and women, too. It has helped me *immensely. Immensely*, because therapy helped me rediscover the person inside of myself I had hidden for so long. When I was married to my alcoholic wife, you make excuses for their behavior. You don't go to social events, because you're afraid of what she's gonna do. You end up crafting a whole other life separate from her, because you can't stand to be around *her* life.

Now, some people would ask, "Well, why didn't you just dump her?" *Easier said than done.* I had compassion, and I wondered what would happen to her if I did. And I was an enabler, all those kinds of bad things . . . 'til, finally, it got to a breaking point. And I said, "No. I'm done."

When I met my girlfriend, Michele, shortly after that time in my life, as I said already, I hadn't addressed my issues, and it affected our relationship. My not dealing with those issues wasn't good. I wish I had. But I didn't, and I'll live with that. Besides, looking back is a bad habit.

Dealing with your mental health is not a 90-day program where you're cured—whatever that means. It's a work in progress. It's a growth cycle. It's a journey. And I'm so glad I put my feet upon that path. I started writing a journal. I'm posting my "Cowboy Wisdoms" again. I started back doing a lot of stuff I had stopped doing when I was going through my tougher times. Truth be told, I don't post *political* crap anymore, because I don't care to. I want to inspire folks with a little wisdom I've picked up in my life.

Overall, though, I'd rather post things that make people think or make 'em feel good that day, instead of the political stuff. Hell, there's enough politics already.

Writing in my journal allows me to combine my *spiritual* life with my *mental health* life. Every now and then, I look back on some of the stuff I've written and say, "Wow, look what I've said that has changed over time (or *hasn't* changed over time)."

It can be hard to deal with all of this, for sure. I think mental health is one of the toughest issues we're dealing with in this country. I've been glad to see NFL football players and other public figures talking about it, talking about mental health. That's because we *all* go to dark places sometimes, and if we don't seek help, it could lead to addictions and places even darker than we ever imagined we would.

It's also clear that mental health and physical health go hand-in-hand. That's why, when I moved down to St.

George, when I first started working on myself again, I knew I had to work on my *whole*, *total* self.

That's just what I did, including talking with people about what I was going through and what I'd *gone* through just as I'm doing now. I think if more people did that, well . . . we'd all be a lot better off. And happier.

COWBOY WISDOM

Life is not a dress rehearsal. This is it, so give it your all now, and don't say, "I'll do that later." "Later" is too late.

The only constant in life is change. Don't resist it. Embrace it.

"Success" is just *failure* that has learned the right lessons from its mistakes.

RESILIENCE

It's not how hard you fall. *It's how well you bounce back up.* You have to be able to recover from situations, whether it's riding your horse and you get bucked off, you lose a job or a girlfriend or even if somebody dies. You can't keep dwelling on it. You can't keep feeling sorry for yourself. Resilience means something happens, and you know it's an opportunity for you to be *tested*. If you have resilience, you have the ability to say, "Ah, shucks!" and get back on.

You ever heard of Bob Stoops? A good football coach. He used to coach Oklahoma.

Well, Bob wrote a book called *Don't Let Them Beat You Twice*. If his team lost, he'd go in the locker room with them and tell his team, "All right guys, we lost today. Y'all got fifteen minutes to feel sorry for yourself. Then we're gonna start thinking about our next opponent."

What he was trying to tell 'em was: If you dwell on it, your next opponent's gonna beat you, too, 'cause you'll still be thinking about this game you lost the week before.

I've written about that before, and it's important to me because *that* is resilience.

"Shake it off!" like we used to say, or, you know, "Rub some dirt on it!" Worry about the things you *can* fix. What you *can* fix is how you react to the *next* situation.

It's true in every aspect of life—whether it's romance, whether it's the death of someone close to you, losing your job, *anything* that may happen to you: you *have* to be able to get back up. I tell you something else, too: I think that's a very *American* thing.

This kind of resilience is something very special about the West specifically. All the cowboys I've met, all the ranch folks I've met: they've all got this brand of resilience. Shit, these are the people who get up in the morning, and if the weather's bad, their whole day just got ruined. They might have planned on doing *one* thing, and all of a sudden they gotta worry about *another* thing.

A fence breaks, or a tree falls down, or there's a fire or whatever it is. But these cowboys and these ranchers have to keep going anyway. And you know what? There's no way this country could have ever survived if we all quit every time we get knocked down.

After Pearl Harbor, did we quit? Nope. America got up off the deck after being knocked down, pulled together and kicked the Hell out of our enemies.

Now, I'm merely a man. A simple human being like anybody. I'm not perfect. I'm not unfeeling. Have there been there times when *I* got knocked down and had trouble getting back up again? Of *course*. You bet.

There was the time when I divorced my second wife, who suffered from her inner demons. My dad had just died. My mother was dead. My brother Rob was dead. I had my two other male siblings and my sister, but they all had their *own* lives and their *own* issues to deal with, you know? So, while I was going through this challenging time, I felt absolutely *alone*. *Totally*.

I was also getting ready to move to Idaho, since I'd *left* my wife and filed for divorce and needed to find a new place to live. I needed cataract surgery then, too. So, I got the surgery, and for a few weeks I saw the best I had since I was in the first grade and got my first pair of glasses. I was packed and was going to leave for Idaho. I went to ride Beamer, since he wasn't going to be joining me for a few months while I got settled. I was loping around the arena, and then suddenly my left eye went half black. "Oh, shit! What's going on here?" Turns out I had a detached retina.

Going through all of this, and I had *no one*.

I was lucky enough at the time to have found a temporary place to live in, a wonderful studio apartment above the garage on the ranch of this nice couple I knew.

They more or less took me in and made me feel like family. That was when I detached my retina and had only 48 hours to operate before there would be long-term serious damage. I'm sitting there at the ophthalmologist's office 50 miles from my home; *"How am I gonna get home?"* Well, the folks in the community out there where I'd been living were great, and some of them came to pick me up and pick up my truck.

The next day, they dropped me off where I would get my surgery, and then I'm lying there *scared to death*. I had *nobody* to talk to on either side of me, too, because they had curtains up separating the other patients. I could hear a man talking to his wife on one side. On the *other* side, I could hear *another* guy talking to *his* wife.

These two guys I couldn't even see but could hear—*they had somebody there with them, but I DIDN'T.*

It made me feel that not only did I not have anybody with me right then, but that I was alone in the world *overall*. *I got* nothing, I felt. My *marriage* had just fallen apart. I had a house I had to pay a mortgage on. It was all almost too much.

One morning shortly after my surgery, I was lying in bed and feeling sorry for myself. *What should I do? What should I do?* Then I remembered what my mom had told me about, something that had happened to *her* when *she* was a young girl. Her dad had brought her to California, hacking and coughing the whole way, because he had black lung from being a railroad engineer. She had secured a job as a domestic for a family. She was only about eighteen and alone in the world. She told me that one night she had looked in the mirror of the small room she occupied and said to herself, *Well Jeanne it's up to you now*.

I remembered that story and remembered that, in the end, it's all up to *you*. You've gotta find that resilience inside of yourself. There I was, at my lowest point. But I had to sit up in that bed and tell myself, *Get off your butt, Patrick!*

I went down to tell Bob and Carolyn, the couple who had rented me The Nest as they called it, and I said, "I need to tell you something. I'm done feeling sorry for myself. I'm moving back into my house. I'm gonna get my stuff outta storage. I'm gonna get back in the game. I knew it would be a long road back.

That's resilience.

COWBOY WISDOM

Faith is believing in something even when the going gets tough and you think you can't go on. But more than that, it is believing in the Man upstairs to get you through it when it does. Having a great horse to get you through doesn't hurt!

FAITH

One of my favorite Christmas movies is *Miracle on 34th Street*. Maureen O'Hara is a department store marketing person who is responsible for getting the store's Santa Claus hired. She has lost her faith in many things. But the Santa Claus she hires restores her faith. He is the "miracle."

She is a single mom who has raised her daughter, played by a young Natalie Wood, to not believe in Santa Claus because she doesn't want her kid to grow up believing in such childish things. At one point toward the end of the movie, after she has had her epiphany about faith, Natalie Wood asks her, "What's faith, Mommy?" And Maureen O'Hara says, "Faith is believing in something when everything tells you *not* to."

That is faith.

You wanna step out over a hole, a *bottomless* hole into the unknown? What makes a person take that step? You're gonna fall down in there forever, aren't you? But a person who has *faith* may believe that he or she can step right on over the hole and be fine—the way we see Indy take a similar step toward the end of *Indiana Jones and the Last Crusade*.

A person maybe will pray or will perhaps think real hard on it, and take that step, take that leap the way Indiana Jones did to get to the other side of the endless crevice between him and the next tunnel he had to get through to make it on the rest of his perilous journey toward the Holy Grail.

Indy *must* get to the other side so that he can use the Grail to save his father's life. Rather like what the German philosopher Kant said: "I *can*, because I *must*."

So, Indiana Jones takes that step (believing that he'll make it across, as foretold in the scroll he uses on his way to the Grail), and he *makes it across* to the other side. He takes a deep breath, takes his first big step . . . and he makes it all the way over the seemingly bottomless crevice below. *That's* faith.

Really, it's a lesson for *all* of us. You gotta believe that you're gonna make it and go for it. You gotta keep telling yourself, "I'm gonna make it." No matter if it's because you have faith in God Almighty or whatever else it might be. You gotta find your own way on the road to faith and follow it.

We see this even in something *like* Alcoholics Anonymous, where people come to terms with the fact that they're alcoholics and that they're gonna have to put one foot in front of the other, one day at a time, and live the rest of their lives like that.

That's how *I* live. One day at a time, having faith that if I simply keep taking those steps forward, I'll get to where I'm supposed to be going. For me, it's my faith in God that sustains me.

I've said it before, but I'll say it again (and I'm *not* the one who came up with it), "Sorry looks back, worry looks around and faith looks up."

"Sorry" means you keep looking backwards, you keep saying, "Oh, gosh: woulda-shoulda-coulda." You're looking backward, and you don't even realize that that's doing nothing for you. You get stuck in a *cycle*. You're just standing around, walking in a circle. You gotta get *past* that. You may be scared about taking a new job, but you gotta do it. You may not want to get back on the horse after having fallen and fracturing your pelvis like I did. Well, at some point, you need to get right back up again. The way to get over regret, worry and anxiety like that is by *having faith*.

I think more people out there are rediscovering faith, because they're realizing more and more that there are some things you can't explain through science or logic. You just have to have faith.

We've also gone through a long time of *losing* our faith, too. We have lost faith in our government. We have lost our faith in *each other*. 9/11 came and brought us all back together again but then it didn't take long for us to go back into our corners, hollering at each other once more. Because we don't have faith in each other.

Look, I was *in* politics. I *know* it's a bunch of skunks and charlatans. But the politicians and their consultants are *responsible* for what's happened to us in this country. They destroyed our faith in each other. Winning elections and not fixing problems is their goal.

Which is *why* I'm glad to see that, as I said, a lot of people are rediscovering faith again. They wanna have faith in *something* outside of themselves, and many are returning to faith in God. They wanna believe in something greater than themselves.

Even Gen Z is rediscovering faith in God after being raised in a secular world.

You know in 1966, *Time* magazine had a cover that said in *BIG* letters, "IS GOD DEAD?" Turned out they were wrong.

COWBOY WISDOM

Don't let your yearnings get ahead of your earnings. Or, as Mother used to say, "Wantin' and gettin' are two entirely different things!"

The rich man isn't the one who has the most. He's the one who needs the least.

**A man might have three houses,
but he can only sleep in them one at a time.
And in the end, he'll be sleeping in
the same sized box we *all* will!**

WEALTH

Money and wealth are necessary evils. You're gonna have to have it if you're gonna live.

Me, I've never been so adept at acquiring wealth. What I have now is not much, but it's probably gonna get me through to the end *if I do it right*. If I make some more money, well, that's terrific. (I'll probably just buy another horse anyway!)

I never saw money and wealth as the most important things in life. To *me*, the most important thing has always been my wanderlust, my search for who I am and what my purpose in this world is.

Which is why I never really buckled down, so to speak, and got that 30-year job. Heck, I took the LSATs for law school, and I did pretty well. But, I didn't *want* to go to law school, you know? In my main profession—communications, PR and that sort of thing—the only way you learn how to do it is by *doing it*. By the seat of your pants.

I believe that's still true today.

Experience is what counts in that field, and in so many others, too. Which, once again, probably goes back to why I've never acquired much *monetary* wealth.

Do I wish I had more? Sure, I do. But would I trade the *wealth* of *experience* I have for the *wealth* of money? Hell, no! Nope, not gonna happen. Whether it was a success, a failure or a mistake, I wouldn't trade any of the experiences I've gone through for a pile of money. *Any* of it.

In looking at the sum total of my life, when I'm gone, I would *much* rather have a church crowded with people whose lives I touched saying their goodbyes than an empty church with a big bank account in my name that won't do me much good by then, anyway.

If you wanna know what I *really* want—if and when I have some real "success," so to speak, maybe on a financial level—it would be: buy myself ten to fifteen acres somewhere, bring my horse, get *another* horse maybe and have that be my sanctuary, you know? May be simple to some, but it's all I want, truly.

May be corny to say it, but *real* wealth to me is my having been able to put out my message to all the people who listened to me when I used to do my radio show. When people would call in and say they loved what I was doing. That made me feel wealthy.

Granted, you could call this ego-driven, but it did feel good to know that there were people listening to me and that they felt like they were part of something greater than themselves and wanted to make sure I knew I was a part of that, too. "You're one of us." That's wealth.

It's like when I write my "Cowboy Wisdoms" and people on Facebook or wherever else tell me they think one of them is especially great that day.

Now, sure, we're a pretty darn materialistic country here in America, aren't we? Boy, don't we all got a *lot* of stuff? I read a quote one time that says we'd all be a lot better off if we didn't have so much stuff. In a way, that's true, ain't it?

It's funny, though, how it used to be that you'd buy a washing machine, and it'd last fifteen years; whereas *nowadays*, you buy one and it craps out in a couple years. They call it "planned obsolescence." It's seems to me that the more we acquire and the more materialistic we become, the *crappier* all that stuff we're blowing all our money on gets!

We've become such a disposable society: *"Just throw it away!"*

Funny, too, because I'm old enough to remember when we had milk bottles that were dropped off and picked up (when empty) by a milkman. They'd take your empty bottles and sanitize them with hot water (and whatever else they used) and then fill 'em up for you again. Everybody's talking about recycling these days, but it was back in the day with that kind of thing when we *really* recycled!

I mean, *Boy Scouts used to collect old newspapers to recycle!*

Regardless of all that, in the end, I'm gonna stick with what I've been saying all along here: I'd rather have the wealth of my life than the wealth of a bank account.

Now, maybe it's easy to say that, 'cause I don't *have* a big bank account, but. . . .

DON'T PRAY FOR THINGS. THE ALMIGHTY IS NOT AMAZON OR COSTCO, AND FAITH DELIVERS SALVATION AND COMFORT NOT PACKAGES.

CSI

FRIDAY

THE COMMON SENSE COWBOY'S GUIDE TO LIFE

MENTORSHIP

POLITICS

ETHICS

PATRIOTISM

SPIRITUALITY

PATIENCE

COWBOY WISDOM

Young fella, I've been thrown out of more bars than you've ever been in!

When a cowboy's too old to set a bad example, he hands out good advice. That's what I try to do every morning. I set enough bad examples in my day!

MENTORSHIP

I've had some pretty good mentors over the years.

When I was getting into politics back in 1987, I got in on the fundraising side. Became a fundraising gypsy, really. Going all over the country doing jobs for different campaigns. Got pretty good at it. Was meeting a lot of very influential people, and they liked me, and they liked my work enough to keep hiring me.

Specifically, I was working for Al Gore at the time, 1988 in California. He was running for president at 39 years old as a southern moderate and was not yet running on his climate agenda. I liked him back then, although I imagine if we met today we probably wouldn't agree on anything.

Though I'd had a *little* experience, basically I got thrown into the fundraising fray.

At one point, my boss in the campaign said to me, "You're gonna meet Peter Kelly. He's coming out to do a trip with you around the state." Peter Kelly had been the treasurer of the Democratic National Committee under Jimmy Carter.

Peter was a smart, sharp and affable man, about six-foot-four, and had a *beautiful* voice. He had been in the world-renowned Whiffenpoofs singing group at Yale. He's a lawyer and political consultant from Connecticut and has vast connections. A wonderful, wonderful man.

He took me under his wing. Any success I enjoyed was because of Peter. When he left California and went back to Washington, the campaign called me and they said, "You are very fortunate."

I asked, "Why?"

They said, "Peter's decided you're 'one of his.'"

That was a real compliment, because he didn't mentor just anyone. He was out there with me to observe and report on me, how I acted in the field, so to speak—how I did my job.

While we'd be out there, he'd also keep giving me tips and lessons about how to approach people for money.

Peter would say, "Don't *ever* think your job is just asking people for a check. They're not giving you money because they have this great view of democracy. They're giving you money because they wanna be an insider. Rich people wanna be insiders."

I'd say, "Hmm."

And then he'd say, "So, remember to get as much information as you can from inside the campaign, so that when you talk to a potential donor, you can go, 'Hey, by the way, here's a little intel on this or that.' This way, they can then go tell somebody *else* that they have inside information and can get them to contribute."

That was early in my fundraising career, and I never forgot his sage advice.

When I got my first presidential appointment at the General Services Administration in the Clinton administration, somebody called me on the phone who I'd raised money with, and they wanted a favor from me. They wanted information on government real estate that I could give him. GSA handles certain real estate. I was green, and I didn't know what to do. But I did know what he was asking was at the very least unethical and maybe even illegal if I gave him the information.

I called Peter, and he said, "Nobody should ever, *ever* do that again! I am gonna call that gentleman, and you'll never be called by him again!"

Then Peter went on to remind me that I had done the right thing. "You didn't knuckle under, and you didn't let him sway you," Peter continued. "I don't care if he gave you ten million dollars. That doesn't buy anything other than your goodwill." I learned a lot from that and a lot more from Peter Kelly for which I will always be grateful.

I've mentored a couple of young people in the communications world.

It was fun, trying to get my mentees to understand that, when you're in the PR business, you gotta be a *storyteller*. People are not hiring you just to take care of the crisis that they're having at the time. They're not hiring you just because they got a new product they wanna push. No, you're supposed to *tell the story*, whether it's a *negative* story or a *positive* story. You have to learn how to *tell* that story. *Their* story. That's what I used to teach young people.

I'd sit with them sometimes, and I'd say, "Tell me a story."

"What do you mean?" they'd ask me.

"Tell me a story from with a beginning a middle and an end." Little exercises like that, that they wouldn't be expecting.

When I first went gathering cows up in Idaho, way back in 2008, I'd never ridden on the range before. I was scared to death. I'd never ridden all day long before. I didn't want to screw up. I didn't wanna look stupid.

I didn't realize that the fact that you're out there with the cowboys *shows* them that at least you're willing, and you're not gonna embarrass yourself. At least not on purpose. They're not there to make fun of you. You didn't sign up to ride a horse with training wheels. You signed up to go do a job. I know that now, but at the time, I was apprehensive for the three days of gathering cows.

When I began to see how I'd been accepted by the cowboys and cowgirls, it really amazed me. We were all out there *together*, doing a *job*. That guidance from them, that sense of confidence from them was what really helped me get over my fear and led me in many ways to becoming a real cowboy myself.

They might not have known it, but they were mentoring me.

Then meeting Trudy was probably the most important thing. It wasn't just about riding the horse. It was all the *lifestyle* stuff. Doing things the "cowboy way." It was all the "cowboy up" stuff. When the group I learned with would be working cows, she'd say to us things like, "Don't ever cut in front of another cowboy, or you're too close to that cow and he's gonna suck back and get behind you!" "Don't do that," she'd say. "You're gonna get in trouble." She was giving us lessons for life that were second nature to her because she had been born into it. *That's* really mentorship right there.

But Trudy did more than mentor me in horses and cows, and the cowboy way. Whether she knew it or not, she was mentoring me in life—*and I think she knew!* If I live to be a thousand, I'll never, ever be able to do enough to thank her for it. Along with her husband, Skip, too . . . *and* her son, Paul.

She is still mentoring and teaching me even if now it's only by phone. I talk to her all the time, and I get excited, because I'll tell her how I did something just as she taught it to me. Then she'll go, "You got it. You know what to do."

When your mentor tells you, "You know what to do, I taught you that," it's probably the greatest feeling in the world.

COWBOY WISDOM

"Just because you don't take an interest in politics, doesn't mean politics doesn't take an interest in you."

—Pericles

"This country has come to feel the same when Congress is in session as we do when a baby gets a hold of a hammer. It's just a question of how much damage he can do with it before you take it away from him."

—Will Rogers

Small minds and big mouths have a way of hooking up. And most of those folks get elected every two years.

POLITICS

People are tired of politics, infecting every part of our lives. 24/7. I sure am, and I don't think I'm alone.

They're not thinking about politics as much as they're thinking about how much they want to see things get done.

They want *solutions* to all the major problems we're facing in this country, most of which are *not* in Washington, DC.

Yeah, I know the media thinks politics is the most important story in America every day, but is it really?

I mean, America is *broke.* But, still, if you think of the country like a house, we need our roof fixed, we gotta take care of our crumbling foundations and deal with the plumbing that *sucks* even worse than the bad wiring. Yet, politicians are out there saying we should build a new pool.

That's real bipartisanship for you.

The biggest problem being we're in a two-party system whether we like it or not. And, in the end, Democrats and Republicans are basically doing the same thing, just in different ways. No matter which way they go, though, *we're* the ones who end up having to pay the freight, you know? *We're* the ones paying the price.

When I think of *politics*, I think of the people I've met in the political world and how it's kind of *two-faced.* Yeah, it's kinda like, *"Go tell the people one thing, and then behind the scenes, make fun of them."*

Yesterday, I was watching the presidential inauguration. And it doesn't matter where I stand on the political spectrum myself—but Trump was *rough.* There wasn't the flowery language of, "Let us go forth to a new world" or that kind of thing. Trump instead said essentially: This is the Golden Age. Here's what's gonna happen. Here's what the last guys did, and I'm gonna fix it. It was *blunt.*

I mean, if I was from the opposition and was sitting there watching this, it'd be like getting hit over the head. I noticed while he was speaking (and I can tell these kinds of things, having worked in DC) that the "Washington types," the *permanent folks* of both parties didn't like what they were seeing and hearing. They were clearly squirming in their chairs. I was watching it on my TV, and I remember thinking, *This speech is not for you guys in Washington.*

Trump took aim and thumped the opposition (both Democrats and the ones in his own party!). He laid the wood to them.

It was and is long overdue.

His *own* people—the MAGA folks, the people who get up and go to work every day—loved it.

In the past, a lot of these people had put their faith in other *politicians* and those *politicians* run, get the vote and—then all of a sudden—they completely forget the hard-working people who put them in office. Then it happens all over again two years later. "You people are the salt of the earth," the politician says to get their vote, and then as soon as they're elected, they couldn't give a shit about the voters once again. Rinse and repeat.

Which is why, to me, it seems there's this massive disconnect between the politicians and the voters, the *People.*

The story of the "Forgotten American" goes way back in our history. Consider Richard Nixon, who won an election talking about the "Silent Majority." Which is also why, whenever I hear anybody talking about Trump's MAGA revolution, I say it's not new. Trump didn't start it, but he understood it better than any other politician in American history.

MAGA is the same movement of "working guys" or "regular folk" birthed by Nixon (and probably before) and midwifed by the Tea Party into the potent movement of Trump.

Politics in the modern world has really changed into something that is invading every part of our lives and larger society these days. You can't get away from it now. Even *sports* is a sector of life that has become infiltrated by politics. Even in movies, they've all got these political messages now.

It seems everything is politicized, and there's no break from it.

I think change is happening, and we might be turning the corner away from all this politics in everything. I sure hope so.

You can't even go to the movies to escape all this bullshit. Disney did a remake of their 1937 classic *Snow White and the Seven Dwarfs*, and it was a politically correct, DEI mess.

Here's a thought for the geniuses at Disney. Just re-release the one from 1937! I'll bet dollars to doughnuts it would make a fortune. God, I hope they don't try to remake *Davy Crockett, King of the Wild Frontier* and rename it *Queen of the Wild Frontier*!

You know, I used to say this on my radio show: One of the great things about America is that we're often conscious of our faults, and we can be self-correcting. One of the great things about America is that ours is a system of government not based on religion.

Ours is a system of government that is also not based upon allegiance to a king or queen. Ours is a system of government not based upon ethnicity either. We're a melting pot, after all.

America's is a system of government based upon pieces of parchment under glass at the National Archives. That's pretty unique. And those pieces of parchment were written in such a way by the Founders and Framers as to say, "Now, we have no idea what's gonna happen years from now, but we're giving you a document, the Constitution, and a method by which, if you want to change things, you have the right to do that, and there's a *way* to do it."

This way, we're always looking forward, always looking to the future. Once we conquered a continent, we began looking up to the stars. There was always something else we could, together as a country, move toward exploring.

It's important we remember this about ourselves as individuals and about ourselves as a country.

That should transcend the politics of the moment.

COWBOY WISDOM

The measure of a man is when he does the right thing even of no one is watching. If you do the wrong thing, and nobody saw you, do it, it is still wrong. And there will always be two witnesses—you and God.

There's right and there's wrong and nothing in between. The only thing between them are excuses. And just because someone might say, "Well, it's legal," ***that don't make it right!***

ETHICS

When it comes to ethics, the first thing I think about is The Ten Commandments. Unfortunately, seems today a lot of people would refer to them as The Ten *Suggestions*. Which just don't read or sound the same, now do it?

When I was growing up, most everybody had some kind of religious training. Not that they went to church all the time, or went to synagogue or temple or whatever, a mosque or whatever it was. But there was always a basic belief in God, a spiritual nature to life.

Even beyond all of *that*, we're talking here about the idea of an ethical, moral background—*the difference between right and wrong*. There ain't no gray.

I've always said that any organization like Congress that feels the need to have an ethics committee *has* no ethics, you know? What I mean by that is: If members of Congress need to go to an *ethics committee* to make sure whatever they're doing is "ethical," then they don't *deserve* to be members of Congress in the first place. You catch what I'm saying here?

There's a similar issue here whenever I hear a politician emphatically say, "That goes against our values." Well, buddy, what *values* exactly are you talking about?

What *really* makes me nauseous is that, whenever a politician says something like this, you never see a reporter drill them about defining those so-called "values." And why is that? Big secret: They don't *have* any values! Even when they *do* try to talk about these values, we have no idea what they mean. Like when Nancy Pelosi said she wanted to "introduce America to San Francisco values." Well, Nancy, what the *hell* do you mean by San Francisco values?

Boy, people are just throwing around words like that now, without having any idea of what they mean. And then, yeah, they're not *challenged* on what they're saying by the press. Which is all part of *why* our society has the morals of a damn alley cat these days. Whatever goes, goes, and if you don't get caught for doing anything bad, well . . . then that's okay, and you're scot-free. In fact, *these* days, if you do something wrong, you're more likely to get a book contract than the consternation of society. Which is *no* damn way to run a society.

It all comes down to the fact that we don't live by the Seven Virtues these days; we live by the Seven Deadly Sins.

Where does this all come from? I'd say part of it comes from the rebellion we Baby Boomers waged against our parents. "They want me to do *this?* Well, no way: I'm gonna go do *that* instead." I mean, wow: just look at our *Sexual* Revolution. We really went wild with that, didn't we?

But what did it all lead to? Today you got *twelve*-year-olds having sex. And I don't just mean necking in a movie theater, but full-blown sex. And, yes, my generation is as much to blame for that since we are the parents and grandparents who allowed this all to happen.

Then you have the fact, too, that the media and the entertainment industry became social arbiters for the next generations. And we all know what kind of morals and ethics *those* folks have! No *wonder* there's so much trouble understanding the nature of truth, reality and a real value system.

Then you have people saying, "Don't be so old-fashioned." That's another term you always hear. Once again, though, *what do you MEAN by "old-fashioned"?*

On top of all *this*, you of course now also have the Internet, which is basically the Tree of Life for a lot of this stuff, a lot of the changes we've been seeing in the newer generations and how they view values, morals and ethics.

One thing about the Internet is that it's got two pipes. One is a pipe that brings wonderful things to us and the ability to find information that we never had such easy access to around the world. It can be a learning tool. But the Internet can of course *also* be a sewer teeming with all the effluence of society.

The answer? We need to clean up the effluvia and promote the good stuff about the Internet. The ability to communicate with other people more easily in many cases: That's good. Having kids looking at porn or TikTok videos all day: that's *bad.*

Much of this once again comes down to the parents and grandparents taking more responsibility to clean up the mess that a lot of us made. For example, if we don't like the crap coming out of Hollywood these days, we should support more entities like Angel Studios, which produces more wholesome stuff.

We need to have some more counter-programming, if you will.

If Hollywood is going to establish a certain narrative today, then we need to establish a certain *counter-narrative* to all that.

A lot of this also comes down to *education.* We need to do a better job of educating our kids in school and elsewhere today, so they can better understand what real morals and ethics are all about. *Real* values. And not just whatever garbage they see on the Internet or in movies and TV shows today that often go *way* beyond the pale in the kind of sex and violence they show.

And if that's "old-fashioned" of me to say, well... guess I'll wear that badge proudly.

Most importantly, we need to instill some common sense in the young people of today and get them away from this herd mentality that has been such a bane to their existence.

However things change, and wherever we go in this society, it will always come down to the three legs of the stool that society rests on: ethics, values and morals. If you take away one of the legs of that stool, the stool will be weaker for it.

Perhaps, then, we should take a note from Mr. George Costanza from *Seinfeld*. There's an episode where George comes to terms with the fact that everything he's been doing in his life is wrong. In an attempt to remedy the situation, he decides that, from now on, he'll do the *opposite* of everything he's been doing. And he succeeds!

Maybe that's what *America* needs to do. We're in such a bad place right now with ethics, morals and values that maybe we should do the *opposite* of everything we're doing right now. Because, heck yeah: The stuff we've *been* doing just ain't working.

COWBOY WISDOM

Tell me there's no pride left in this country, and I'll tell you to go to a rodeo.

PATRIOTISM

Growing up in post-World War II, early Cold War America, patriotism was, from the get-go, when you first stood for the Pledge of Allegiance to the flag coming over the loudspeaker every morning in school.

Then, I remember being on the Safety Patrol. We manned the crosswalks around the school. We had red jackets, and white Sam Brown belts and these yellow caps. To be on the Safety Patrol, you had to be a good student, you had to show up early to school, and you had to do all kinds of other things, too. And one of the things you had to do was take down and fold the flag every day.

You didn't pull it down like a janitor does nowadays and throw it in a box. Instead, you brought it down slowly and steadily, with a kind of reverence, and you folded it *properly* before putting it away. We had to *learn* how to fold the flag correctly.

It may sound like a small thing, but it was part of learning patriotism. It was the America we grew up in.

Maybe it was because a lot of our teachers were World War II veterans. Maybe it was because of the Cold War going on, with everybody being worried about the Russians and our other enemies. We had to be unified as a strong country.

Now, a little later, the Vietnam War changed that. It really changed things a lot. You'd hear stories about the disrespect Vietnam veterans had to endure when they came home—getting spat upon and all that. They'd come home and want to get in civilian clothes as soon as they could. A national disgrace.

Nowadays, if you're wearing a uniform around, everybody walks up to you and says, "Thanks for your service." At least we didn't repeat the mistake of a different time. But that is a form of patriotism as well as respect.

I will say that you don't have to wear your patriotism on your sleeve. Patriotism should be in your heart, it should be in your mind, it should be about internalizing the idea that you're privileged to live in this beautiful America.

That all said, do we as a country have faults? Of course we do. But when I hear people who say, "Well, look at slavery." I just think, *Do we really wanna judge ourselves by where we* were *150 years ago or by how far we've come?*

I also believe there's too much of this attitude of people who think, *You're not a patriot if you don't believe what I believe.*

That's not being a patriot.

Being a patriot is loving your country for all of its mistakes *and* for all of its successes. Looking in total at what we have and what we've become. And also understanding that dissent is one of the basic rights of the country. Our country was *founded* on the right to dissent.

I wish we could get back to dissenting without *labeling* each other and *hating* each other. I do think it's possible. I really do. I think people are starting to realize that we've gone too far with certain things. That we've spent all kinds of money we didn't have, we've allowed ourselves to get too politically correct, and maybe we need to get back to basics before AI takes over!

When it comes to cowboys in particular, the root of patriotism runs very deep. You go to *any* rodeo, and you'll see that patriotism. God and country.

Cowboys know that America gives them the freedom to do what they wanna do, to *be* cowboys. America gives them the freedom to follow their dream. It gives them the freedom to own a ranch, to ride out there *forever* if they want to, if that's all they want to do.

That's the *beauty* of the West: When people came out this way from the East, they came out here seeking a better way and the freedom that was guaranteed to them by the Constitution. The freedom written down in the Declaration of Independence—*life, liberty and the pursuit of happiness*. All of this is *why*, in the cowboy world, patriotism runs so deep.

And that's why, when you go to *any* rodeo *anywhere*, there is that moment when the announcer asks everyone to stand as a young woman comes riding into the arena making the big circle with Old Glory fluttering from the pole she is carrying for everyone in the crowd to see and to honor. I don't care if it's a small rodeo in Carey, Idaho, or the National Finals Rodeo in Vegas, that part of the show's the same.

People take off their hats, and the announcer leads a prayer. Yep, God and country. They stand up straight and proud for "The Star-Spangled Banner." You'll see little boys with their hats over their hearts. Little boys of three and four years old, because *that's what they're taught*: respect for the country, belief in its principles. And most of all, that ability to do what you wanna do. Not just "willy-nilly do-what-you-wanna-do," but the freedom to *pursue your dream by following the rules*.

It doesn't matter if your dream is to be the number-one cowboy in America at the NFR or if your dream is to own a small space and have a nice wife and a few kids and raise some cows. *Whatever you wanna do*. Whatever gives you that ability to realize those dreams. Now, *that's* patriotism.

COWBOY WISDOM

"It is time we learn to steer by the stars and not by the lights of every passing ship."

—General Omar Bradley

Doin' the Lord's work don't pay much, but there's a wonderful retirement plan.

SPIRITUALITY

You know, for a while, I kind of drifted astray. I didn't pay much attention to my spirituality for a long time. Maybe because I was having too much fun, or maybe it was because I didn't really care. I can't tell you why.

Think about it: You're in your twenties, and then before you know it, you're suddenly in your thirties and then your *forties*, and you're focused on your job. Then think about it some more: You have no kids that you're trying to educate in the ways of what some might call their "faith" or just some general spiritual nature, some belief system. So, you just end up setting this "faith" or spirituality aside.

That was me. I was focused on my job, on my "career," and there just wasn't *time* or what felt at the time like the *need* for that kind of "faith" *or* spirituality.

Then you get older still, and I guess at least for me, at a point, I realized maybe I've been missing something. Maybe that has something to do with the fact that, like a lot of other folks, the closer I get to the end, the closer I want to get to God.

Though this may not be true with everybody, it certainly has been the case for me.

Now, I like to think that, for all the cowboys that I've been around, faith *itself* is extremely important. All you gotta do is go to the rodeo and watch the bull riders kneeling before they get on the bull. Then there's the fact that every rodeo conducts a public prayer—everybody's standing up, men reverently taking off their hats and placing them over their hearts.

It's like, "Wow! Here's guys on horseback. Guys standing near the chutes. They're holding their hats over their hearts, because it's important to them."

They're praying because in this very real moment when they're about to climb aboard a 2,000-pound bull, they rely on the protection of the Lord. If you ever get the notion to ride a bull, you *better* be praying before you hop on!

It's humbling, considering the notion of faith being so crucial to the life of the cowboy and the cowboy lifestyle.

Is it a "going to church" kind of faith? Of course, it *can* be, and you know something: there *is* a thing called "cowboy church." Cowboy churches can be a *lot* of fun. There's usually music—country-style music and hymns, and you can get some pretty good fire-breathing preachers there. Everybody's wearing cowboy hats and boots, and not because it's a costume; it's because *that's what they wear every day*.

There's also a great cowboy poet and singer and songwriter named Red Steagall, and he has a song called "Cowboy Church." But *his* cowboy church is *the great outdoors*. *His* cowboy church is sitting on his horse and seeing everything that God created and still marveling at it every day. And knowing that he doesn't have to be in a building to pray. He doesn't have to be in a building to have a chat with the Lord—if he wants to pray for healing, or pray for forgiveness, pray for a good crop, pray for more rain.

That's the kind of spirituality I've forged as my own.

I do pray every morning and every evening now. It feels so soothing to start and end the day that way. I'm up at five o'clock and start the day giving thanks for that day in particular: "Thank you, Lord, for letting me rise again. Thank you for letting me experience this day and experience this life, which is the gift you have given me, the most precious gift." There's a lot more to it but that's the idea.

So, again, I think that's kind of the Western way, the cowboy way of doing it: You say it in your own way, sure. *But, you darn well say it.* There's the way of experiencing it, maybe during formal situations when people go to church in the traditional way. But then there's *other* ways of experiencing it, like just this morning when I was sitting on Beamer, and there was nobody here, and I just marveled at it all: "What a beautiful life I have here. I'm sitting on the most precious thing in my life." Beamer really *is* my salvation these days. And thank you, Lord, for entrusting me with his well-being and for his love and the solace he gives me.

There's a lot of cathedrals in this world, but I don't care how fancy the building is or what kind of vestments the clergy's wearing. No matter what religion we're talking about, it all comes down to faith, your beliefs and trusting in God.

That's really *my* deep spirituality, and do I think it's the spirituality of the West, along with a lot of cowboys and cowgirls.

COWBOY WISDOM

Patience is not the ability to wait, but the ability to keep a good attitude while waiting.

Taking care of a horse is a journey of patience, love and lifelong companionship.

PATIENCE

Well, *patience* is one of the great virtues that we often forget. We've become a country that's always in a hurry. In fact, I would say throughout our history, America's been a place that's always in a hurry, always wants to get things done quickly and move on to the next thing.

It's also true that, in our individual lives, it's real tough to tell kids that they should *wait for things* and *put in the work* and *think good things will come* and *be patient*. Instead of instant gratification, which is what a lot of people want, more people should be going for *delayed satisfaction*.

That can be hard to consider, because, for a lot of us, our *wants* and our *needs* can often be two different things. And *wants*, just as often, tend to be those things that we *want* right away. I guess it's in our nature to be a nation in a hurry. Maybe that's because of our newness on the world stage.

The *good* news is even though we've been around for 250 years almost, that doesn't seem to stop us from wanting to fix the world.

The *bad* news there is that, because of the fact that we like to have things done quickly in this country, we can be impatient. The American people, after they've voted in their candidates during an election, they immediately say to their new political leaders, "Why haven't you done anything yet?"

Now, I'm not absolving the politicians of their responsibility *to* do something—because they've been pretty bad at it for quite a while! But we *do* need to do a better job in this country of recognizing that the wheels of government don't move fast.

Some of our impatience, of course, comes from the advent of technology. Just consider the notion that instead of having to go to a library and spending all weekend there going through stacks of books, now you can just look up a lot of what you need on your phone to write your term paper. So, that kind of thing is going to make us more impatient, and that's something we're gonna have to deal with.

I also think these advances in technology also make it that much harder for parents to teach their kids *about* patience. Although I'm not a parent myself, I do know it's very important that we teach these kids that there are no shortcuts in life. It's just hard to deal with for *all* of us, now that patience is probably the most common virtue that has become so *un*common in today's world.

One of the exercises I go through to work on *my* patience is, when I'm sometimes talking to Beamer, trying to get him to do things we need to do that day, I'll stop myself and realize that I can't raise my voice and expect him to right away do whatever I'm asking him to do. He has no idea what my words mean. But he does know my tone of voice, and I need to exhibit patience.

I tell you: *It's the same in ANY life situation*. You can't keep looking at the situation that you're in and blame the *situation* for you're not getting the result you want. You've gotta look at *yourself* first. It's too easy to "blame the horse" (so to speak)—the horse being a metaphor for the situation that you find yourself in. If I'm getting impatient with Beamer, he won't do what I'm asking. And we're not gonna accomplish anything in our session that we're trying to accomplish.

There was one time when I was trying to get Beamer to do something we needed to do, and (I don't know why; maybe I had an appointment that afternoon or something?) I kept looking at my watch and was basically trying to *force* my horse into doing what I needed to do. Or at least what I *wanted* to do. It wasn't working out the way I wanted, and so I stepped back, I told myself to *wait a second* and to stop being in such a hurry.

"You came here to do something," I said to myself. "And the fact that Beamer's not doing it the way you want, it means you're not asking the right question, that *you* might be doing something wrong." And being impatient to boot.

I would suggest that *anyone* going through a similar situation step back and examine *yourself* in the situation you're facing there. You have to ask yourself, "Am I doing this the right way?" You gotta take a deep breath and then think to yourself, *What* is *the right way?*"

There's the old cowboy saying: "It's the *work*, not the *clock*, that tells you when it's quitting time." Which means that you can't just say to yourself, *I gotta go do something, so we're gonna go real quickly*. No, you do that and your "horse" is not gonna respond the way you want. See what I mean?

In the case of my *actual* horse, Beamer, as soon as I figured out what I was doing wrong, he then did what I needed him to do *perfectly* a couple of times, and it was like, "Wow, that was on *me*. I was impatient. I didn't understand what my situation was, and I should have let the situation dictate more of what I was doing rather than my *watch* telling me I have to go do something else."

SATURDAY

THE COMMON SENSE COWBOY'S GUIDE TO LIFE

SELF-CARE

RELAXATION

POETRY

REPRESENTATION

GRIEF

COURAGE

COWBOY WISDOM

When the going gets tough, the only person who can solve your problems looks back at you in the mirror every morning.

SELF-CARE

When I was younger, I was like Peter Pan. I thought I was gonna live forever and that I could do whatever the hell I wanted to do, including drinking too much, going out all night and all that other stuff. I didn't worry about self-care. I didn't think much of it.

It wasn't until I returned to California from Washington, DC, that I really began thinking seriously about self-care.

When I left the Beltway in 1997, I was in horrible shape, absolutely *terrible* shape physically; I was older than my years. It was then that I started going to a 24 Hour Fitness to get back into shape.

I got myself a private trainer who was a bodybuilder. He eventually became Mr. California. Believe it or not, he kinda talked like Arnold Schwarzenegger (though his accent was a little different, because my trainer was from *Armenia* instead of *Austria*). He'd say things like, "We take you down, now we build you back up!"

At one point, he even suggested I enter a senior bodybuilding competition, but I didn't want to go *that* far with it all. (Eating only broccoli and chicken breasts for twelve weeks straight? No, thanks!)

Before this, I also wasn't thinking *anything* about life or death—nothing spiritual, nothing about my emotional or mental state. I just let all that stuff slide. Occasionally, I would look up to the heavens and ask, "What the hell's going on with my life?" But I wasn't yet taking any of it seriously, and I never looked for something to help me get through it all.

As I said (here and elsewhere in this book), my sanctuary really became riding horses. In a way, they became my teachers for my self-care. It became everything about being with them—their *smell*, the *feel* of a horse and the love.

The whole experience of riding horses helped in so many ways. For instance, sometimes you go in to get your riding lesson, and you give them your check, you leave, and that's that. But, me, I prefer to get to know those people and have them get to know *me*. So, it stops just being, "Here's the check, see ya." And it starts becoming more like, "Hey, how's it goin' today? What've you been up to?" And we even up becoming friendly. Whenever I can, I try to develop more of a relationship with these people. I guess that comes from my wearing my heart on my sleeve.

But, anyway, chatting with the people at the lessons helped me break through to taking my self-care more seriously, too. Their asking me if there was anything at all I wanted to talk about when I came in was extremely helpful with all of this.

After a while, as I met different people and rode different horses, I got to Beamer and then eventually Trudy, and they in a way became my de facto therapists. They could *sense* when something was wrong, and I really appreciated that.

That was partly why my riding lessons and events became more and more important to me. It was why I even started *praying* again. *Clumsily*, but nonetheless trying!

There was a woman who'd be at the competitions that Trudy would organize who'd conduct a prayer. We'd do prayers before events like they do at rodeos.

So, this lady would do the prayers, and we'd all take part in them. But then she eventually stopped coming out, because she was very busy traveling and doing many other things. Which is about when Trudy asked *me* to start doing the prayers. She just *sensed* I could do it. And I did, and everybody would bow their heads and listen. I got pretty good at it.

That really started me even more so, not only on my self-care but also on my getting back to my spiritual side once again.

There's a sign I have in my home office that reads, "Don't look back. You're not going that way." I don't want to worry so much about what I did or didn't do in the past; instead, I want to focus on what I'm going to do in the *now* and in the future.

I don't know *where* I'll end up settling in the end. Maybe Colorado. Maybe Wyoming. I don't know. But I'm glad to be in St. George, Utah, these days, even though I can tell you that this more than likely is *not* where they'll be burying me. For now, though: guess it's Utah. As I told my therapist, "Moses got thrown into the wilderness. Jesus went into the wilderness. But this here in St. George is my wilderness where *I* came to in order to get myself right." And, I tell you, it's been working out great so far.

I've been able to see the change even in my broadcasts on Newsmax. I'd been doing those for a few years, but I have to admit that I got to the point where I was kinda phoning it in. When I started really looking at myself and working on my self-care, though—on my mental, emotional and physical health, my appearances got much, much better. There was even a young producer at one point who saw the difference, too, and told me, "Wow, you've really been *popping* onscreen lately!"

It feels so good that I feel strong enough to really be the best version of myself for me *and* for other people, like my friends or family when *they're* going through hard times. That's life for you: *It sure ain't easy*. But that's why I'm so thankful I've figured out how to pull myself together, even this late in life. Because, here's the thing: It's *never* too late.

Like everyone else alive today and who's *ever* been alive, I don't know how much longer I'll be around for. But however long that may be, I just wanna make sure I'm doing it the right way.

I tell you, as a person, you have to look at yourself and ask, "*What can I do to make myself the best version I can be?*" That is self-care for sure.

COWBOY WISDOM

If you want to have a drink or two, that's all right. But don't wear out the soles of your boots on a brass rail.

RELAXATION

I discovered the "old guy at the end of the bar" during the late '70s and early '80s when I was living and working in San Francisco. In fact, I met many of them. I learned a lot from them.

These were the last years of what I'll call "old San Francisco," before all the new technology took over and no cell phones. San Francisco was really a bunch of different neighborhoods—some ethnic and some by whether you were working class or upper crust. It was really a small *town* in many ways, which happened to be made up of a handful of little neighborhoods all bound together to make a city. In the working-class and middle-class neighborhoods, there was a neighborhood bar on almost every corner. I'd head out to those places a lot back in the '70s and '80s, because they were like little living rooms. It was how I relaxed and met people.

No phones buzzing on the bar, no running tabs with a credit card. You would order a drink, put down your money, and the bartender would make change and put it right in front of you. If you went to the bathroom, it would still be there when you got back. We also played dice for drinks, and the sound of the dice cups hitting the bar was a familiar sound in most San Francisco bars.

You had your own neighborhood bar where you could walk to and leave safely on your way home. They also became like living rooms because there was an earlier time when television was new and still too expensive for everyone to have one, and, so, people would go to bars to watch sports or whatever might be their pleasure, together with their neighbors.

On top of *that,* many of the apartments around there were small and confining, and, so, getting out to the neighborhood bar was, yet again, a way to have something of an expanded living room for people who didn't want to feel stuck in their tiny domicile all night or on the weekends.

Then you've got other amenities like a pool table. Then there's other people there who know you, like in the theme song from *Cheers*: "where everybody knows your name. . . ."

I've always liked that to do that, and I must say I took to it like a duck to water. Popping into a bar, having a few beers, maybe a whiskey. You know everybody, and they know you. Maybe you get lucky and there's some good live music, too, like in a place I used to go to called Mulcrevy's where there was often accordion player belting out old Irish songs. I got to know Bob Mulcrevy and his wonderful wife, Gracie, very well. It was like family. And I loved every minute. It was great. A lot of fun.

I wouldn't go to places like that to just drink and party, because bars like that were, yes, like an expanded living room for me, and I was a well-known local character. And *oh*, was I a character! We were *all* characters there.

There was one bar, Perry's, that was a bit more upscale but still a neighborhood bar with one of the most wonderful and colorful collections of San Francisco characters you'd ever want to meet. Male and female. I fit in pretty well.

I knew all the bartenders and waitresses and even busboys. My favorite was Michael McCourt, a ruddy-faced Irishman. If you looked up "Irish" in the dictionary, Mike's picture would be there. His brother was the author who wrote the bestseller *Angela's Ashes*. Mike was a legend in San Francisco. And in a hard-drinking town like San Francisco was in those days, that's saying something! Mike and I became friends, not close friends but friends nonetheless.

Just like Norm on *Cheers*, I even had my regular stool whenever I went in. And if Mike was working, he could tell right away if I had been "over served" the night before, and he knew what *medicine* to prescribe to get me right again. One Sunday, with my *San Francisco Chronicle* tucked underneath my arm and my Camel cigarettes, I wanted to watch the 49ers on TV and there was this couple sitting on the stool I used regularly. I joked to Mr. McCourt, "Hey, Mike, What's going on here?" And he proceeded to nicely inform the couple that they needed to move because that was my seat. We'd have a colorful little back and forth, and they moved. I bought them both a drink. And then Mike administered the medicine in the form of a shot of Irish whiskey—one more for me *and* one for himself, too!

It was a grand time.

But more than that, I think this kinda thing is important, because *we all need a pressure valve release*. Like all the adventures of my life, that period taught me a lot about human nature and how to get along with all different kinds of people. You realize that people are people, all shapes and sizes, and color or religion don't mean a hill of beans. It was my first real experience of living in the American melting pot and learning how to work and play among different folks. It has served me well.

Walking the streets of San Francisco and being recognized by friends or hanging out in the neighborhood bars was a form of relaxation. We all need a way to relax, take it easy and have a good time. You don't want to overdo things too much. (*And I had the hangovers to attest to what happens when you do!*) But we all need something that gives us pleasure. A place where people can go to laugh, meet new people and, again, take a load off from a hard day, and forget your troubles.

And where every one knows your name.

COWBOY WISDOM

Don't let so much reality in your life that there's no room left for dreamin'.

POETRY

There's something called "cowboy poetry," which is really more or less a brand of storytelling in poetry form that tells of the life of the cowboy, the rancher, the horse trainer, ranch wives and ranch life and life on the range—*all* those kinds of folks and situations.

There are events all over the West and Texas where cowboy poetry is celebrated. The granddaddy of them all is the National Cowboy Poetry Gathering, held every January for the last 40 years in Elko, Nevada.

There are poetry recitations and workshops to learn cowboy stuff, from writing poetry to braiding rawhide for reins and other tack and even hat shaping.

And there are cowboy music concerts.

I finally made it there last year for the first time after years of saying I was going—and then didn't for one reason or another, but that's another story!

There was a woman at a concert—maybe 80 or so—by the name of Yvonne Hollenbeck, and she told stories about being a ranch wife, and it was beautiful poetry, with standard rhyming and all that.

Still, it was just a *story*. One that was funny as hell, I might add.

There were some people sitting there with us who didn't quite understand what this woman was talking about 'cause she was talking about *ranch* stuff, and there were those there who aren't ranch people. They like to come to these meetups because this type of storytelling and cowboy poetry is part of an American cultural tradition.

Yvonne reciting her cowboy poetry was *great*. It was so awesome the way she was talking about her "Top Ten" list of things that a ranch wife *doesn't* like to do.

Then she told stories about her husband and how, even though they love each other very much, they don't give each other Christmas gifts anymore. It started a while back when they were raising their kids, and, the way ranch life goes, sometimes beef prices are up and sometimes they're down. And they didn't have much to spend on each other.

So, one year, he was asking her what she wanted, and she had seen this silver ring she wanted from a jewelry store in their small South Dakota town. To keep things fun, of course, she didn't want to come right out and say that's what she wanted, so she told him she wanted something silver and round that she had seen in the corner window.

Christmas rolls around, and what does her husband get her? The silver and round item *he* had seen in the corner window of the *hardware* store: a silver dog bowl. In full fairness, he'd thought she was tired of just dropping the dog food off on the floor, and they both had a good laugh about it.

She had some other funny stories she told in poetry form, too—about sorting cows with her husband and all these other ranch life things. I'm laughing my head off, and the poor guy next to me has *no* idea what the poetess is talking about or why I'm laughing so hard because I don't think he knew much about sorting cows!

One thing that came through with all her stories was how much she loved her husband, her family and the life she lived. You could just tell she wouldn't trade a minute of it for anything in the world.

In addition, you can hear cowboy poetry in cowboy *songs*. Not to be confused with *country* songs. No, those are two different things. *Cowboy* songs are pretty distinctive. And there are a lots of fantastic practitioners of them—the late Don Edwards and Chris Ledoux, Red Steagall, R.W. Hampton, Trinity Seely, Sons of the San Joaquin, Riders in the Sky and my personal favorite, Dave Stamey and countless others. Cowboy songs tend to be written and performed by real cowboys and tend to focus on life on the range, horses, romance, all mixed with happiness for the cowboy life, sadness at the tragedy of death and breakups and wrecks and in many cases the love of the Lord and Jesus, much like cowboy poems.

My *favorite* cowboy singer, as I said, is Dave Stamey, and he is, first of all, a cowboy, obviously. He used to pack horses in order to deliver supplies to people who needed them in the mountains. And his songs tell these stories about that kind of lifestyle . . . once again, in really funny ways sometimes and serious at other times.

There's a lot of humor in cowboy poetry and songs, because cowboys often have to see the humor in even some of the bad things that go on all the time out there on the trail or in the rodeo arena. That's where so many great cowboy poet/singer witticisms come from. The attitude really is one of, "If it doesn't kill you, it's funny."

Cowboy songs, like cowboy poetry, tend to be not only funny but plain ol' *fun*, too. But a lot are also very serious. Ones about love, for instance. There's cowboy songs where the cowboy has to choose between the trail and his girl. There's one by Dave Stamey called "Old Red" about a bronc that "couldn't be rode" and a cowboy who'd "never been throwed." And the cowboy gives Old Red a try, but the bronc flips over, and they both die.

There's a cowboy song by Red Steagall about a guy who's very proud of his son, because his son is working with him. He may have a pricey mortgage, and things may be rough sometimes, but his son is right there by him, and that gives the guy pride.

There's another song by Red about a fella who wakes up in the morning and gets all mad at the whole world, because cow prices are down and he has to sell some of his cattle early. But then, to cope, he starts going over what is *good* in the world and all his blessings, which include the fact he's got a good dog, a good woman, a truck that starts and a friend with a trailer in case he needs to haul his horse anywhere.

So, there's definitely different kinds of cowboy songs about all sorts of topics. And it's simple stuff. But they really are *beautiful,* too, because they are about people who look life in the eye and face it down. Largely because they have no choice. They've chosen this lifestyle, and they *love* this lifestyle; they wouldn't give it up for *anything.*

The people who write these poems and songs, who *perform* these poems and songs are *survivors*. They've survived everything that's been thrown at 'em, whether from mankind or from Mother Nature. They gotta get up in the morning, they gotta get the work done. It's a hard life, but they love it.

What really makes it *poetry* to me is that they are putting themselves in God's hands. They're out there working the land, and, as one rancher I met once said, "It's not *my* land and it's not the *government's* land. It's *God's* land, and I'm just takin' care of it for Him for a while. Then after *me*, someone *else* will take care of it for a while."

It's *poetry*, because it's the story of these people and their lives. It's an American saga.

I bring in some cowboy poetry style a lot of the time when I give speeches. I might present what I have to say in a laconic cowboy style, and I might make people laugh in a way where what I'm saying really sinks in. Since, as you know, I didn't *grow up* a cowboy and didn't get into the life until much later down the road, I see myself as something of a bridge between those who have always lived the life, and those—like the fella next to me who didn't get why I was laughing so hard—who haven't.

You want my opinion? I do think we've become too damn serious as people. I do think we should laugh a little more and loosen up. It's the way to get through tough times.

Listening to poetry or songs, particularly when they're about what you're going through—and maybe *other* people who have gone through or are going through *themselves*—can make a big difference in how you go about living your day.

And I tell you something else, too: We used to be much *more* of a storytelling people, and I do think that cowboy poetry and cowboy songs—especially with the great mixture of humor and pathos—help tell stories in a way we still really need to hear these days. Maybe now more than ever. Certainly much better than stories of all these superheroes or about how many people can be crushed by a Transformer or whatever it is!

Cowboy stories are the last vestige of the true oral tradition in telling America's story and the story of the cowboy who helped shape that story.

COWBOY WISDOM

"The cowboy's way of life and earthy approach to survival have been an inspiration to kids and grown-ups in all nations of the world."

—John Wayne

"This is the West sir. When the legend becomes fact, print the legend."

—*The Man Who Shot Liberty Valance*, 1962

REPRESENTATION

A lotta times, people ask me what I think about the way cowboys are portrayed onscreen. Now, as I keep saying, I didn't grow *up* a cowboy, even though my mom grew up for part of her childhood and teens on a ranch and would tell us kids all about it when *we* were growing up.

So, it definitely had a major impact on my life as a small boy even before I got into the cowboy lifestyle. Especially because of the special bond my mom and I shared. After all, she named me after her father.

At the end of my mom's life, she was in the final stages of dementia. And I'll never forget the time right at the end, when I was with her and asked how she was doing. She looked right at me and said, "We gotta go get the horses. The cows have gotten out. You gotta get the horses. Go saddle up my horse and go saddle up your horse. We gotta get going, Patrick."

She was saying it with such *clarity*. Then she kinda drifted back and away again. It was at that moment that so much of what she had told us about her "cowboy life" came back to me, all that cowboy wisdom she had raised us kids with. This was a woman who took part in a cattle drive at *75* after having not ridden for almost 50 years!

It was like she had been putting all this data in my head, all the old cowboy sayings, and all the little cowboy stories and all that stuff.

Still, I didn't get into all this *myself* until later on in my life, and I still am learning and have a lot to learn.

That all said, I do know a lot of people like Trudy, and other friends, who have helped me get to where I am, and they certainly know what they're talking about when it comes to the cowboy life. And they always tell me plenty about it.

But let's go back to when we Baby Boomers were kids. Or even a little further back to the days of *radio* shows when there were series like *The Lone Ranger* and *Gunsmoke* (before it went on to become one of the most popular television shows of all time).

When we were kids in the 1950s and '60s, our Saturday mornings were filled with nothing but cowboy shows.

There was *Fury*, which was "the story of a horse and the boy who loved him." There was *My Friend Flicka*, there was *The Gene Autry Show*, there was *Roy Rogers and Dale Evans*, and *Hopalong Cassidy*.

This was also around the time that my mom would give my oldest brother money to take himself and the other three of us boys to the movie theater on a Saturday. There were "serials" you'd watch before the main feature, and at the end of each installment, they'd tell you to *come back next week for the next exciting episode.*

These were mostly westerns that were basically morality plays—the good guys versus the bad guys.

That's the kind of thing we grew up with.

Later on down the road, westerns moved onto stories where the main character was an *anti*-hero. Clint Eastwood and *his* characters in Sergio Leone pictures. Then movies like *The Wild Bunch*. Westerns became something different at that time. Even John Wayne, when he got much older, ended up in a movie like *True Grit*, where he played a character who was not very much like his earlier, more traditional archetypal "good guy" characters.

No matter where the westerns went with the kinds of characters they showed us onscreen and where they went with the stories, and the tone and style the cowboy heroes or anti-heroes usually still had a code they lived by. There was always a lesson for us kids growing up, and throughout our time getting older—the idea that a *man's gotta have a code*, he's gotta have a creed to live by. I still very much believe in that today. (It's really a lot of what this entire book is about!)

Right now, today, we're seeing onscreen the stories about big ranchers, like what Taylor Sheridan has been doing with the extremely popular show *Yellowstone*. That man's done a great job with what he's done, no question about it. He's brought a lot of awareness to ranching, to the West and all the rest.

Interestingly, I think what makes the show work so well is that, really, in the end, *Yellowstone* is all about *family*. Which brings us right back to older television shows like *The Big Valley* and *Bonanza*.

Like these later movies I've been talking about, *Yellowstone* is different from these earlier series, because a lot of the main characters are not all good guys. Some of them are very unsavory characters.

Nevertheless, they're all still fighting the same battles and going through a lot of the same things and dealing with a lot of the same themes as shows from back in my childhood days.

I'll let you in on a little secret: I have an idea for a TV series of my own, and it too would be a western, of course. But the difference *here* would be that I'd be talking about the folks in the cowboy and ranching world who *get lost in the shuffle*. The little guy. The *little* rancher we don't really see too much in movies or TV shows. The smaller cow-calf operators, ranchers with smaller operations who may have to sell off their calves early, because they need to get whatever price they can to survive.

It's a part of the West we haven't really seen much of onscreen before. And I think it's important to show this unseen part of the story—people who are doing whatever they can to get by. People who are all over little towns scattered around the West have gone through some really hard times over the last few years.

Many of these little towns have yet to recover from economic downturns and other problems, such as natural disasters.

Or think about these logging towns in California that got hit hard and have also never recovered because urban environmentalists decided they knew more about the forests than the folks who'd been managing them for generations. Me, I wanna see more of *those* stories. Maybe one day, I can help tell 'em.

But, yes, there's the idealized life of the West and the cowboy, and then there's *also* the hard realities of what that life is really like out there.

I think it's important to show *both* sides of things, because there are moments when I'm out there watching the cowboys do what they do, and they have everything thrown at them—weather, banks, bureaucracy, illness, whatever—and, yet, they keep going. They keep standing up for what they're doing, and they keep doing it.

It reminds me of what the actress Jane Darwell, as Ma Joad, says toward the end of the 1940 movie classic *The Grapes of Wrath,* The adaption of John Steinbeck's novel of Okies heading to California during the Great Depression: Pa Joad says to her, "We shore have takin' a beatin'." And Ma says, "I know, maybe that's what makes us tough. Rich fella comes up, and they die, and their kids come up, and they ain't no good, and they die out. But we keep-a-comin'. We're the people that live. Can't nobody wipe us out. Can't nobody lick us. We'll go on forever, Pa. We're the people."

While the Joads aren't cowboys, they possess the same toughness and spirit and grit. You could just hear those words from a rancher's or farmer's wife.

To me, that *is* the West. That *is* "the cowboy." It's everything I've ever observed of these men and women. They *have* to be tough, and they *have* to be resilient, because it's one thing to lose a *job* and to be trying to find another one, but it's a *whole other thing* to lose an entire *lifestyle,* which is what "the cowboy" is—not *just* a job.

We need to remember that and see more of that in the films and TV shows about 'em.

We need to see 'em deal with all the ups and downs of that lifestyle.

Through it all, no matter how they appear onscreen, I tell you: They *will* keep going, hopefully, and even if their lifestyle may in some ways seem like it's vanishing somewhat, it *is* still there for now. And I'm hoping it stays for quite a while longer. *However* people portray or view 'em.

COWBOY WISDOM

Most of the stuff folks worry about never happens. Worrying wastes the most precious gift we have all been given: The gift of *time*. Don't use up one second of it worrying about something that might never happen.

GRIEF

The one thing that I would tell people about handling bereavement is: *Don't be alone*. Don't isolate yourself. Certainly, take some private time for yourself and think about that person. But don't do it sitting in a dark room. Go do it outside somewhere. Maybe go to a place that you know that person liked, and try and get in touch with them and your feelings that way. You don't have to be a person of faith to do this (although it helps, I think). Whatever you do: *Allow yourself some time to grieve personally.*

Don't go drink way too much just to get the memories out of your head. The person died, the person is gone. But, hey, they were gonna go one way or another someday, you know?

I would also then say that you should try reconnecting with the people who were close to you and the person being grieved. If there's people you have in common with the person—family, friends—reach out to those people, and share stories of the one you are grieving.

When I lost three childhood friends seemingly all at once, but actually over about two years, we "survivors," if you will, all got together for a memorial service in Marin County, where we all had grown up. It was wonderful. Each one of us got up and said something about all three, and we laughed and we remembered their lives and shared fond memories, but it was bittersweet for sure. But what mattered at that moment were their lives and how we all had come together as friends so many years before.

When my dad died, I drove back from the funeral to where I was living and rode my horse, 'cause it made me feel good. It kinda gave me some peace to be around animals, 'cause they don't judge you. Your horse looks at you and licks your hand. He wants another treat. But it gave me some solace.

Again, I would tell people not to get maudlin. You may even wonder, *Gosh, was there anything I could've done?* No. There's *nothing* you could've done. We are born, we live, and then we die. And the world goes on, even after someone you care about deeply is no longer here.

Then *your* life goes on, too. If the person you're grieving could tell you one final thing, they would tell you, "Keep going, *keep going*."

Ranch kids learn about death real early. The calf dies, the dog dies, the pig dies, the chicken dies. They learn early about the cycle of life. What goes along with that is the fact that there has to be an *acceptance* of that on their part. If a horse breaks a leg, you gotta put it down, right? It's hard, but you gotta do it. You gotta put 'em out of their misery.

So, there's that feeling there of, *"We gotta keep going."* We can *mourn*, but we gotta keep *going*. Once the mourning's over, it's time to cinch it up and *keep going*.

You watch one of those old movies where there's a cattle drive, and sometimes one of the cowboys gets killed. What do the other guys do? They bury 'em. They put a marker over the hand-dug grave and take off. They *gotta* keep going, because they're on a job and they have to *complete* that job.

When I was ten years old, it was 1962: the Cuban Missile Crisis was threatening nuclear war. We all knew what was going on, even though we were just a bunch of kids. We talked about it in school and everything. There was, of course, a great fear in America.

I remember going home and talking to my mom, telling her how scared I was. *"Mom, we're all gonna die!"*

And she sat me down, and she said, "Patrick, I'm gonna tell you something. *Everybody's* gonna die."

I looked at her, and I said, "Even you?"

"Even me." Then she added, "Now, the quicker you learn that, the quicker you can get on with the business of living."

I will never forget that.

To this day, I remember how she looked at me when she told me that. She was a comforting mother, but she was also stern enough not to just fall back on, "Oh, you poor, little thing!" No. Instead it was, "This is life. This is what's gonna happen." It's something I had avoided for a long time until recently when I came to terms with it and understood, finally, that it's gonna happen—that *that's life*.

I think a lot of my acceptance of death has to do with my journey back to God. That has been my salvation and comfort. I'm ready, come what may, because I trust in His timing and His plan for me.

I would like to think someone remembers *me* after *I'm* gone.

It's been a helluva ride—so far!

COWBOY WISDOM

Nobody is born with courage although we have it in us somewhere. It comes out when we face our fears and conquer them.

A person must meet fear to know courage.

COURAGE

The first thing that comes to mind when I think about the famous John Wayne line of, "Courage is being scared to death but saddling up anyway."

I mean, whatever your fears might be, you have to overcome them. After all, we *all* have our own fears, don't we? But, tell you what: In a lot of cases, like in a war, if you're a soldier, the battle has been scheduled, your officers are heading off to the field, and you don't have much choice but to proceed. You gotta go forward, prepare yourself and, even though you're scared, you have to do your duty and face your challenge.

Now, I'm not saying courage means you do something *stupid*, right? You don't want to be *reckless*. No one wants to ride with a reckless cowboy.

Lemme tell you about the time when I was on a mule ride on New Year's Day in Zion National Park. (Yeah, that's the kind of life I'm leading these days.) Now, I've never been much of a fan of heights. And I knew that, when we set out on this mule ride, we'd be traversing some hills and that kind of terrain along the way. (I should add that I'd never ridden a mule before, either!)

Sure, I could've come up with some excuse at the last minute and decided not to head out with the folks I was going to be riding with. I could've called them and said, "Ah, well, you know . . . something's come up." *Instead*, I said to myself, "No. This is 2025. The new year. And I'm going to overcome my fear of heights right here and go do what I said I was gonna do. I gotta face up to this."

And so we're riding on our mules. We're going up this dry wash, which is starting to narrow. I'm looking ahead and seeing that we're going upward toward what will be a *further* narrowing trail. The mule, *he* knows what to do. He's surefooted, smart. Mules actually know *exactly* what to do if you trust 'em and just let 'em do what they're doing. But as we were continuing to head upward, straight up, my cinch—which we had already tightened before we left—somehow came loose.

I had to figure out what to do, because there were people coming up behind me. And there was no place to stop, nowhere to pull over to get off and tighten my cinch.

I had to keep going. There was no choice. So, I just had to balance myself left and right in the stirrups to keep the saddle in the center of the mule, because if it rolls to one side, there's too much weight on one side of the poor mule.

We finally got to the top of the trail and had some space to spread out a bit and rest for a moment. I told Paul, my friend and optometrist who owns the mule, that my cinch was loose. He came over and went, "Oh, my God! It is!"

I tell him what I did to stay balanced, and he continues, "Yeah, that's what you gotta do." I did what I was supposed to do in what was actually something of a dangerous situation, because I stayed firm, overcame my fears and dealt properly with the problem at hand.

Of *course* I was scared. But it was what I like to call a "respectful fear." I was being *respectful* of my fears—acknowledging them, understanding them and being brave despite that—without being reckless or stupid in how to *handle* those fears.

I can't remember who said it, but they say that *fear's a great motivator*. The positive side of all this is going back to my concept of "respectful fear." There will *always* be times where you're gonna say to yourself at some impasse, "Wow, this is gonna be *difficult*." But if you don't face your fears, you'll never be able to *do* difficult *things*.

As I've said in one of my past "Cowboy Wisdoms," *life has risk*. You can't regulate, litigate or negotiate your way out of every problem. Sometimes shit just happens, and you gotta face whatever you're going up against, learn to *deal* with it.

Something else to consider here is that bravery and courage have their *roots* in fear.

Some guy wins a Medal of Honor. What a brave guy, yes? Look what he did! Jumped on a hand grenade and saved his platoon, or went charging off into a machine gun nest. With the odds fully against him. Brave!

Yes, but also he was scared. He had the choice to either remain there in the foxhole and let the enemy come get him and potentially his platoon, or he could have said, *Fuck it* and go do what needed to be done. That's courage, that's bravery.

A lot of it is about defying that voice in your head telling you to just stay put and *not* charge out into the unknown. It's negative thinking like that that would've kept our early settlers and pioneers from moving west across the Great Plains and crossing mountains as they forged the country we have today. You gotta ignore that shit and keep moving forward.

I tell ya somethin' else, too: When I was on that mule ride? There was a four-year-old girl riding along with our group. She got bucked off . . . *twice!* Her father was on another mule, and he calmly got off both times, and both times he didn't panic. He didn't run to her in desperation, "We're gonna quit! Let's get outta here!" No.

This little four-year-old who got bucked off the mule picked herself up, cried a little bit, dusted herself off and let her father put her back up on the mule.

And, boy, I was right behind her! I saw her get pitched both times! But here was her dad teaching this *child* courage and self-reliance all at once. It's that perfect lesson of, "You get knocked off and you get right back on again." You know something? That little girl's gonna be one of the toughest lil' cowgirls you're ever gonna see in this world of ours, because she had to face her fear and got right back up on the mule both times.

That's how ranch families do it. One of the kids falls down or falls off a horse or whatever it might be. The parents don't go running out frantically and put bubble wrap around their children. They don't make 'em wear helmets everywhere they go or put them on those darn ridiculous leashes some of these parents have for the kids.

Instead, they say, "Okay. You're gonna be all right." They check for broken bones or check to see if anything is actually wrong, and then when they see everything's fine, they help their kid back up on the horse, and then it's *back to work*.

That's what so much of bravery and courage come down to. That's the point I've been trying to make here. We *all* get scared. There'd be something wrong with us if that weren't true. But *you gotta worry less and work more*. Gotta face your fears and work your way through it. *That* is how you can *truly* find your courage.

That's what it means to "cowboy up." You fall, but you get back on the saddle and get back to work.

You teach *that* to your kids, and *that's* how we build a strong society.

THE GOOD LORD GAVE US EACH A CERTAIN NUMBER
OF SECONDS, MINUTES, HOURS, AND DAYS,
BUT HE DIDN'T GIVE US OUR EXPIRATION DATE.
USE YOUR TIME WISELY, AND LIVE LIFE TO THE FULLEST.

CSI

SUNDAY

THE COMMON SENSE COWBOY'S GUIDE TO LIFE

THERAPY

DEATH

FUTURE

COWBOY WISDOM

Learn what's important and what's not. Then focus on what is, and don't waste your time with what's not!

Life may be *simpler* when you plow around the stumps. But your furrows will always be crooked. It's better to *remove* the stumps. *Remove* the things that block you from plowing ahead.

THERAPY

John Wayne once said, "You'll never find a cowboy on a psychiatrist's couch."

Well, *okay*, but think about famous cowboys or rodeo stars who *drank too much*, which probably led to a whole lot of other problems. At some point, a lotta these guys gotta quit that shit. They were no good to anyone if they were shaking so bad they needed a drink or a drug to steady them. Sure, a lot of 'em turned to God and Jesus Christ, right? There's even Cowboys for Christ, a big group that includes sobered up cowboys who turned to Jesus for salvation because they had so many demons they needed to have exorcised. Or think, too, about country music stars whose lives became a big mess from alcohol, like Johnny Cash, Waylon Jennings, Trace Adkins or Glen Campbell.

A while back, when I got my copy of *Western Horseman* magazine in the mail, there was an article about this very thing. The title was "Things We Don't Talk About in Western Culture."

It was the story about a true cowboy, Justin Reichert and cowgirl Nicole Grady, who started a group for their fellow cowboys and cowgirls to address the issues of mental health, addiction, depression and alcoholism that are found in cowboy culture just like it is in society as a whole.

Justin said," We simply don't talk about it." He went on to say, "We're not taught to process our emotions. We're not taught to talk about our shit, so we don't really know how, and I think a lot of people are going through this, a lot of men especially, and then cowboys are even worse."

That cut deep as I've struggled with many demons in my own life, alcohol included.

Then, what exactly do we *mean* when we say "therapy"? A group like Cowboys for Christ is a *kind* of therapy, ain't it? May not be on the couch, but could have a similar impact for some, no?

Now, yes, in the "old days," you just sucked it up when you had issues. That was back when the John Wayne quote meant you should be tough and not show emotion because that spelled weakness, and no cowboy wanted to be considered weak.

But it's the twenty-first century now, and there's more options to figure out how to take care of yourself. Therapy just happens to be one of 'em.

Even *I* can go back and forth about this kinda thing. Right now while writing this, I got on a shirt that reads, "Rub some dirt on it." Or, you know, there's the saying, "Put some tape on it." Easy fixes for your problems. And there's some humor with those statements, and in the end, when you fall down, you gotta do what's best for *you* to get yourself back up.

Nervous laughter about an old saying on a t-shirt can mask bigger and deeper problems.

If you feel the best way to deal with *your* demons is through going and seeing a professional you can talk to, go and do that. If it's a pastor, or a therapist or group therapy session or AA, then maybe that's what'll work best for *you.* These are all, in their own way, forms of *therapy*.

We can all live like old-fashioned, tough-it-out cowboys if we want. But living by those principles may not be all some people need, and when it comes to the *inner* side of your life, you may need to access other tools like therapy to deal with whatever you might be going through.

Because we *all* must deal with our demons. We *all* got 'em. If you don't think you do you've got even bigger problems.

I'm not ashamed to say that I'm dealing with *mine.* Hardest decision I ever made was to seek help. It was also the best decision.

Part of the therapy journey to me is teaching yourself how to live your life and address things that you should have addressed a long time ago but didn't for whatever reason. Maybe you were scared. Maybe you were embarrassed. Maybe you were ashamed. Maybe you weren't really aware of the demons you were dealing with. Maybe you were hiding. Or maybe you thought it made you look weak. This last one is especially common for men.

We all need people to help us through these times, and—yes—even for cowboys, that may mean your partner out on the range while you're riding and working.

Say you got these two cowboys out there on the working cows. When they take a break, one might turn to the other, "How you been since your wife died?"

His partner: "Dang, you know: It's tough. I don't know what to do."

"Well," the first might ask, "You wanna talk about it?" Ain't nothin' anti-cowboy about that.

That's just two friends, two co-workers out there talking about life. But, to some, it is also a form of therapy.

It's another one of these things we gotta teach to kids: Even if you're self-reliant and completely well-adjusted, it doesn't mean that something else hasn't intruded on your life. You can be the most self-reliant person in the world and still have a wife who leaves you, or you drink too much, or your kid dies, somebody gets cancer, can't pay the mortgage. All things you gotta deal with. Cowboys included. (And *nobody* is so perfect that they have no problems. God spreads 'em out to everyonc.)

That's when you *can't* just rub dirt on it. You *really* gotta deal with it. You gotta *face* it. And it's not gonna be easy, and it's not gonna be the kind of situation where you can just "suck it up" or "shake it off."

That's what we gotta teach kids these days—that there are times when we *all* need help and we *all* need somebody to talk to.

Seeking help doesn't make you weak. In the end it will make you stronger.

And that goes for cowboys, too.

COWBOY WISDOM

Yesterday is gone, and no one is promised tomorrow.

The Good Lord gave us each a certain amount of seconds, minutes, hours, and days. But he didn't give us our expiration date. Only He knows that. Use your time wisely.

"It ain't dying I'm talking about, it's living. I doubt it matters where you die, but it matters where you live."

—Gus McCrae, *Lonesome Dove*

DEATH

I was pretty lucky growing up, in the sense of never really having to deal with death.

Al my grandparents were already gone by the time I was old enough to really know what was going on. In fact, my *mom's* parents had been dead for a long time already. Her father died when she was eighteen, and her mom died when she was a small child. So, I never really *had* grandparents around from either side.

On my *dad's* side, *his* mother died when he was a boy. Then his father married again, and *he* died when I was only about three years old. So, no memories of *that* granddad either. No grandparents at all around the house, and therefore no grandparents dying.

It wasn't until my brother Rob passed away that I first really had to deal with death. It has been twelve years now.

It wasn't sudden; I can tell ya *that*. It's not like he got in a car accident. You know, "Your brother just got in a car accident, and you gotta come out here." No. Not like that at all. My brother had ALS, and when you receive that diagnosis it's a death sentence where the only thing you don't get is the date and how much time you have left. It is harsh and unforgiving.

It sounds crazy, but, yeah: I was in my *fifties* the first time I had a real experience with death. Perhaps it sounds even crazier still, but I never wanted to believe it. I avoided it *completely*: death. I avoided it, because it *scared* me to think about dying.

But it was my brother here who was going, and I of course went to go visit him. I have a video of him that he taped for the ALS Foundation of Las Vegas of which he had become an active member, helping to raise money for them and stuff like that.

And you know something? What you can see there in that video is his outlook, his faith and how *strong* he was.

Nobody wants to die. But when Rob got to the point in his disease where they wanted to put a *hole* in his throat so that he could live longer (he'd have to be kept alive *artificially* with a breathing tube and all that), he said, "No. I've made my peace with God. I'm made my peace with life."

Rob said that he didn't want to be around *just to be around*. That was *so* like my Rob to say. It was such a brave moment.

I wish *I* could've been so brave. Because when, shortly after that, one of my *other* brothers, Steve (who was kinda handling things for Rob), asked me if I wanted to come down and say goodbye when it was getting close to the end, I said no.

For one thing, I didn't wanna see Rob at the end of his dying process. We were too close. He was too important in my life. I didn't wanna see that. I wanted to remember him as my hero. My champion who had taught me how to stand up and be a man.

Secondly, I didn't want to ruin the memory I had of the last time I'd seen him, when he was still at home with his wonderful wife, Lori. My oldest brother, Peter, and I were both there in Rob's beautiful Las Vegas condo. We all watched reruns of *The Honeymooners* together. A whole *bunch* of 'em. Then Rob's wife had to take him to bed in the other room where he had been sleeping toward the end, because that's where they had all his equipment like his CPAP machine to help him with his night breathing and all that.

Lori then came out and asked us if we wanted to go spend some time with him. Rob had the TV on, and since there was no real place to sit, Peter and I crawled up onto the bed with Rob like we used to when we were little boys. And Rob says, "So, what do you fellas wanna watch?" He had the clicker in his hand, and could still use it even though he was very weak.

He's flipping around the channels, and I'm thinking maybe he'd stop on a cowboy movie, like a John Wayne picture or something. Instead, he comes upon *My Fair Lady* and goes, "We're watching *this!* Any objections?"

Then Peter and me: "Nope!"

So, here's three grown men lying in a bed together like little boys, watching (and *singing* along to) *My Fair Lady*. That was my last memory of him. It's the one I want to keep. And I'm glad that I get to keep that.

The next time I dealt with death was with my mom. Wait a second! No. You know something? My mistake. My mom was *before* Rob. My *mom* was my first real experience with death. My mistake!

Anyway, my dad called all us kids (though none of us was a kid anymore!) and told us we should come down and say goodbye. My dad stood by my mom's bed, identifying each of us, because she couldn't really see us by that point. But that one wasn't sudden or a surprise, either. She had had cancer three times, and she was 89 years old. So, it didn't shock us when it happened.

Even still, I cried.

My dad had an aneurysm at 99 years old. Even though he was in great shape and everything else.

We all went down there together to go fulfill his wishes per his advanced directive. And we each got time to go sit with him for a moment. Then it was time, and they disconnected everything. Typical for my dad, he kept hanging in there, though. At least until the next morning.

During my last moments with him, I had told him, "It's time to rake the leaves, Dad." It was fall, the time of year when, because we grew up with a huge yard, we kids always had to rake the leaves. Not much to say, I guess. But it was all I could come up with at the time. And then he was gone.

I sometimes wonder why I said what I did. But then I think that my dad would be happy that at least I remembered something that needed to be done!

As with the *rest* of his life, my dad went on his own terms. In fact, he predicted what was gonna kill him. He'd told my brother Steve, "I've outlived all the cancers and everything else. I'll probably have a brain aneurysm, and that'll be that." Sure enough, *that's what happened*.

The important thing to remember, I think, is that, as you get older, the way I am right now, you start thinking of your own mortality a heck of a lot more. It can be scary, because you realize (as my mother used to say) "you got more winters than summers left."

There's something, I have to admit, that's a little comforting about that. Because death is something coming to us all, it's something we all must face. And there's something about *that* that makes me less afraid of death than I used to be. I guess you could say, then, that I'm more resigned to it than fearful of it at this point in my life.

I've come to terms with the fact that my time is limited.

I'll just have to trust the Good Lord on this one.

As the years start to click by, you realize the reality that years are adding and not subtracting. From the day you are born, you're adding years. There's no time subtracted for good behavior!

Being a good person doesn't mean you *can* stop time or gain more time in your life. No. *Being a good person* just means you get to live the life you have to the fullest and look back with pride that you lived it well.

That's another thing: I'm less scared now, because I feel I've led an interesting life, and I thank God that He's kept me healthy enough that I can enjoy it. And I hope to enjoy it for as long as He will let me.

Me, I don't wanna end up sitting in a rocking chair or in one of those places where you're just playing bridge or bingo all day eating pudding and Jello. I wanna die with my boots on. I don't wanna die any other way.

Now, over the past few years, because of everything I've gone through, I do consider my journey of faith and the fact that I'm much firmer *in* that faith. And, you know, it *can* make me feel a little better about dying and death. I'm trying to be strong like my brother Rob.

Or as strong as my mom, who, whenever we'd ask her what she thought Heaven was like, she'd say, "Well, nobody's come back to tell us what it's like. So, I'm assuming it's a nice place."

I like to believe that. And I like to believe that, at some point, I will be able to see Rob and my mom and dad again. And everyone else who's gone, too. But, then again, to quote the old famous cowboy saying, "If there ain't no horses or dogs in Heaven, I'll just go to Texas!"

COWBOY WISDOM

If you want to see the future, don't gaze into a crystal ball, instead, look into the eyes of a child.

The more promises you make today, the more excuses you make tomorrow. So, don't make promises you aren't ready to keep . . . and keep the promises you make.

There ain't nothin' new under the sun.

FUTURE

When I think about the future, one of the first things that comes to mind is *excitement*.

I'm *very* excited about the future.

If you want to see what the future holds, look at young folks. They're the ones that will create it.

A primary reason why I feel excited is that I've met a lot of young people recently, and they give me great *hope* about the future.

Sure, it's gonna be a *totally different* future from the future when *I* was their age. For example, the young woman who cuts my hair, she calls herself the "Tatted Barber." She's got great tattoos (so do I, for that matter!) *and* she is a little entrepreneur. At 23 years old, she has her haircutting business with a lot of clients.

She developed a beard oil grooming product for men's beards, 'cause she's an *excellent* beard trimmer. She also gives an old-fashioned shave. She's developed the whole thing on her own, and she's put together the marketing plan and is using social media to sell it.

Now that might seem small to some, but I think this is just the beginning for her. She will be successful at anything she tries because she knows it's all up to her to win in life and she is investing in herself.

And she is one of millions of young folks.

No, these young people today are a totally different generation from what I've ever seen before. They will leave a mark.

And don't judge Gen Z by the kids with worthless college degrees hollerin' in the streets. They are *not* the future of America. The reality of life and as soon as Mom and Dad's money runs out they will face a harsh reality.

Professional protesting doesn't pay that well, and they gotta eat.

Bet on the ones who went to trade school instead of college. It's a safer bet.

It does give me great hope for the future.

I used to be like the cantankerous guy at the end of the bar thinking about the youth of America. *"You kids don't know shit, and you don't know how the world works and, boy, you're gonna find out!"* That was a lazy analysis. And I apologize to them.

Instead, now I'm learning more and more how these young people are gonna open up a world that I've never seen before. They know how to use all this new technology so well. They're *innovative*.

That's what gives me hope: My hope is always in *people*. I'm not putting my hope or faith in *things*. I'm putting it in the people that are going to create those things(italics). And these young people, I hope I live long enough to see the new worlds they will create. What a time that will be!

Maybe they can even solve some of the problems we Baby Boomers are leaving behind.

Now, of *course* there's *lazy* ones, too. Yeah, there's ones who aren't gonna do *shit*. *Every* generation has that. But I'm just having so much fun in this world I'm living in right now, meeting so many young people and seeing how they're approaching life.

That's why I'm excited. I'm *really* excited. *God damn* excited! (I'm sorry, Lord.) I really am!

I also hope (and I pray) that we never lose the cowboy way. I hope and I pray that the cowboy way of living keeps going.

I do think that, as long as we have people who are involved in it, that future—the future of the cowboy—is secure. As long as there's parents who raise their kids to follow in their footsteps, there'll always be cowboys.

Now, with AI and everything else, you have got huge ranches that are highly mechanized, highly *computerized* with the growing of the feed and all the rest of it.

You know what, though? *People still need hamburgers.* They still need *steaks*. So, again, I'm hoping that part of it won't change.

As long as we have rodeo and cowboy *events*, that won't change.

Or how about Taylor Sheridan? Taylor Sheridan opened up a whole western thing with his television show *Yellowstone*. Really, he's *reopened* it and *modernized* it. I think that he's helped in that respect.

Now, yes, there's a certain *reality* to face, too. And part of that reality is: in 2008, rural America was hit by the economic/housing market collapse much harder than the rest of the country. They got clobbered, and there's a lot of small towns that don't exist anymore. When you drive through 'em, they're little half ghost towns. They might've had a diner, and they might've had a grocery store and a post office. Well, now they're down to just a post office. The people who live there gotta go shopping somewhere else for their groceries and dry goods.

That, *too,* is the reality of the changing world. But as long as there's one cowboy throwing a saddle over a horse, the cowboy life is gonna survive. The *business* part of it is gonna be tougher, though.

It's funny, when I was in Germany as a young man in 1976, I got on the train, and all of a sudden a bunch of people got on dressed as cowboys, like movie cowboys. Like a John Wayne picture jumped on this European train. They were all speaking German. I didn't realize how much the Germans love the Old West. I think it's still true today. They *revere* it. So, I'm hoping that part survives, and think it will.

National Finals Rodeo Vegas is one of the most popular events in Las Vegas. It brings thousands and thousands of people. A lot of them have never ridden a horse before. Rodeos in towns are still very popular *all across* the West.

One time, I lived in Folsom, California, just about 30 miles outside of Sacramento, where the prison is. They had a rodeo on the Fourth of July, and they drove some Longhorn cattle through town, and I knew a bunch of those people, and they said, "Hey, Patrick, you want to help us drive cows?" It was around this time that I had learned to ride.

So, I threw a saddle on a horse they had for me, and I helped drive the cattle through town. After I was done, I rode the horse back to the trailers and dismounted. And I walked around an old section of town, and there's this mother there who's got a big smile on her face. She came up to me and she said, "Can my son stand with you, and can I take your picture?"

I said, "Sure!" I'm dressed like a cowboy, and she wants a picture of her son with me. Why not?

She took my picture with her son, who had one of those goofy little plastic cowboy hats on. He was a small boy, couldn't have been more than four or five. She took the picture and told me, "Thank you very much!"

Then she went on to say, "We moved here from the East, and this is what I always thought the West was. This is really beautiful!" Then she walked away with her kid. And, you know, it made me feel good that here was this mother, and she'd moved from a faraway place, and yet she still loved the lifestyle.

She loved it so much that she wanted her *son* to see it. His eyes were as big as his head when he was looking at all the cowboy stuff. And all that, too, is why I think there's a future there.

The cowboy way definitely has a future. It's too much a part of the American character and American soul to all of a sudden disappear.

The National Finals Rodeo every Christmastime in Las Vegas has never been more popular. And the retail extravaganza known as "Cowboy Christmas," where you can buy everything real cowboy, big and small, from boots to horse trailers, is almost bigger than the rodeo itself.

Dude ranches have never been as popular as they are now. All these people watching *Yellowstone* wanna look and act like the characters on the show. I read a story a few months ago about how even people in New York City were buying cowboy hats more and more.

I actually talked to a hatter I know who confirmed for me that, yes, people in the cities and suburbs are buying and wearing cowboy hats. They've maybe never been to the West in their lives, but they're still buying these hats in droves! So, I know the lifestyle is still there. And it'll always be there as long as, like I said, one cowboy's or cowgirl's throwing their leg over a saddle.

The only warning I have, and threat I see, is if the city slickers and developers from places like California continue to move to places like Montana and turning the landscape into condos and mini-ranches, driving out the real ranchers and bringing things like their politics and way of life.

But as long as there's cows out there to rope and round up, brand and ship, there'll be cowboys and cowgirls around in the future to come.

So, I look to the future with optimism. I might not be around to see it, but I'm pretty dang sure it will be in good hands.

DON'T WASTE TIME THINKING ABOUT
WHAT MIGHT HAVE BEEN. PUT THE
"MIGHT HAVE BEENS" IN THE SAME
TRASH CAN RESERVED FOR THE "WOULDAS,"
THE "SHOULDAS," AND THE "COULDAS."
THEN GET BUSY WITH THE "DOIN'."

AFTERWORD

HAPPY TRAILS . . . TILL WE MEET AGAIN

It's been a good life. And even though I'm running out of sunsets, I look forward to enjoying many more sunrises in the time I have left.

I see the bartender is getting ready to close.

If you want to hear more, I'm right here, every night, just the old guy at the end of the bar.

See you next time.

And remember . . .

**Wisdom comes from experience.
Most of it bad.**

THE COMMON SENSE COWBOY'S 12 RULES FOR LIFE

1. The secret to a long life is getting up every day with a purpose. Young or old, working or retired, everyone needs a purpose, so find yours.

2. Never betray trust, because trust is like virginity. Once lost, it's impossible to get back.

3. Everything breaks sooner or later. So, learn how to fix things.

4. The measure of a man is when he does the right thing even when no one is watching. If you do the wrong thing, and nobody saw you do it, it is still wrong.

5. Don't waste time thinking about what might have been. Put the "might have beens" in the same trash can reserved for the "wouldas," the "shouldas," and the "couldas." Then get busy with the "doin'."

6. A fancy education might gain you some knowledge, but only hard life experiences will gain you wisdom. A PhD won't help you fix a flat tire.

7. Be wary of the person who tells you they can get you a burger and fries for nothing. There is no free lunch.

8. Your word is your bond, and your handshake seals the deal.

9. If you shake hands with a politician, be sure to count your fingers when you let go to make sure you still have all five. (*See above.*)

10. Don't pray for things. The Almighty is not Amazon or Costco, and faith delivers salvation and comfort not packages.

11. There is right, and there is wrong. There are no loopholes, and the only thing in between are excuses.

12. The Good Lord gave us each a certain number of seconds, minutes, hours, and days, but He didn't give us our expiration date. Use your time wisely, and live life to the fullest.

PATRICK
DORINSON
PSALM 23

ABOUT THE AUTHOR

PATRICK DORINSON (aka the Common Sense Cowboy) has lived through and endured many lives over the course of his seven-plus decades on this planet as a maverick, a dreamer, a schemer and—most appropriately for the purposes of this bio—a communicator.

Dorinson is a longtime author, speaker, and Newsmax and Fox News contributor who, for nearly a decade, was host of his own *The Cowboy Libertarian* radio show on iHeart media's Sacramento-based KFBK.

Although he takes pride in the fact that renowned conservative talk show stalwart Rush Limbaugh had his start at the same station, Dorinson takes further pride still in the fact that throughout his lengthy career, he has worked with equal passion and grit on both sides of the aisle. Along with, as he likes to say, "in the aisle itself."

Aspiring toward being something of a modern-day Will Rogers (with a twinkly-eyed twist of Mark Twain), Dorinson transmits his thoughtful dispatches via his